ARCHITECTURE OF RAIL

ARCHITECTURE OF RAIL
The Way Ahead

Marcus Binney

ACADEMY EDITIONS

For Francis and Christopher

I wish to express my thanks to all the architects and engineers cited and quoted in this book for their help, in particular to Harry Reijnders, and also to Santiago Calatrava, for giving so generously of their time. This book is not a comprehensive survey but a selection of the most remarkable new stations built and designed during the last ten years. It does not include the architecture of underground or metro stations, a parallel subject which would fill another book.
I am also grateful to Academy for their help in publishing *Architecture of Rail*, in particular to Michael Spens, for commissioning my work and for his continuing support, to Iona Baird for editorial input, and to Andrea Bettella and Steven Roberts for designing this book.
Marcus Binney

Cover: Lyon Satolas, Santiago Calatrava; Frontispiece: Lyon Satolas, Santiago Calatrava

Photo credits: **Waterloo International Terminal:** Nicholas Grimshaw & Partners pp12, 14 (below), 18 (centre); Anthony Hunt Associates pp14 (below), 16 (above), 18 (above and below); *New Civil Engineer* p16 (above); Jo Reid & John Peck p14 (centre); **Roissy:** Marcus Binney pp20, 22, 24, 25, 26; **Lille-Europe:** The Grayling Company pp28, 30, 34; Peter Mackinven/Ove Arup & Partners p32; **Lyon Satolas:** Marcus Binney pp38 (centre, below), 40, 42, 44; Calatrava Valls SA cover, frontispiece, pp36, 38 (above); **Marne-la-Vallée:** Marcus Binney pp46, 48, 50, 51; **Kowloon:** Nigel Young pp52, 55; **Sloterdijk:** Sybolt Voeten pp58, 60, 64; **Duivendrecht:** Frank van Dam pp66, 68, 71; **Leiden Central:** Harry Reijnders p72; **Rotterdam Blaak:** Frank van Dam pp74, 76, 78, 80, 82; **Lisbon Expo 98:** Calatrava Valls SA pp84, 88; **Atocha:** Marcus Binney pp92, 96; **Santa Justa:** Duccio Malagamba pp98, 100, 102, 104; **Abando:** Michael Wilford Associates pp106, 110, 111; **Chur:** Kurt Gahler pp114, 116, 118 (centre, below); RFR p118 (above); **Stadelhofen:** Calatrava Valls SA pp120, 124.

First published in Great Britain in 1995 by
ACADEMY EDITIONS
an imprint of

ACADEMY GROUP LTD
42 Leinster Gardens, London W2 3AN
Member of the VCH Publishing Group

ISBN: 1 85490 396 9

Distributed to the trade in the United States of America by
NATIONAL BOOK NETWORK, INC
4720 Boston Way, Lanham, Maryland 20706

Printed and bound in Singapore

CONTENTS

INTRODUCTION

Railway architecture has entered its second great age. This is born of a renewed recognition of the achievements of nineteenth-century railway engineers and architects who gave station architecture a character, and even a vocabulary of its own, through their adventurous use of iron and glass, and then steel and glass.

The revival is prompted by four further factors. Firstly, the advent of the new high speed trains, initially in France, then in Spain and now in Germany. These often run on newly created lines and therefore require improved modern stations on new sites, as at Roissy and Lyon Satolas. At the same time comes the opening of the Channel Tunnel and two spectacular new stations built to serve it – Waterloo International Terminal and Lille-Europe.

The second great impetus has come from the renewed emphasis on improving public transport in many countries, with frequent train services offering an attractive alternative to the motor car not only for commuting but also for shopping, leisure, family outings and school trips. Part of European legend is that Swiss Railways always run on time, but over the last decade the investment leaders have been the Dutch with a spectacular range of improved services, new and refurbished stations and new local services.

The third crucial factor has been the re-emergence of the structural engineer as a creator of station architecture, and the source of the innovative technology needed for daring forms and spans. Three names stand out: the late Peter Rice, whose work is continued by colleagues at Ove Arup in London and RFR in Paris; Anthony Hunt in London; and Santiago Calatrava, who practises in Paris and Zurich and who alone among the leading figures in railway architecture is qualified both as architect and engineer. Anthony Hunt puts it simply;

> ... for the structural engineer, airports, stations and sports stadia offer the most exciting challenge simply because of the clear spans needed.

The fourth key factor has been the flourishing of groups of railway architects notably in France and Holland. In France, SNCF Architects under Jean-Marie Duthilleul has revolutionised station architecture. Duthilleul has been exceptional in giving engineers, especially Peter Rice, the opportunity to develop new structural forms.

In Holland NS Architects, led principally by Harry Reijnders and Peter Kilsdonk, has pioneered a vibrant and colourful new railway architecture, based on close study and appreciation of passenger needs and concerns. As a result of this effort new stations have been voted Holland's most popular modern buildings.

British Rail Architects, the longest established of all, has been effectively disbanded in the run up to the Government's planned privatisation. However, credit is due to British Rail for bringing both Hunt and Grimshaw into the design of Waterloo International. Impressive station architecture can, of course, be produced by outside architects. Proof of this are Santa Justa, Seville, by Antonio Cruz and Antonio Ortiz, the new Atocha Station in Madrid by Rafael Moneo, and Kowloon Station in Hong Kong, now being built to designs by Terry Farrell.

Two key ingredients of the new railway architecture are transparency and colour. Peter Rice, in his last works, became fascinated with exploring degrees of lightness and transparency. On a sunny day the sheer beauty and ethereality of the filtered white light playing on the forest of trusses and girders at Roissy compares with a great pilgrimage church by Balthasar Neumann. At Lille the changes are even more dramatic – on a grey day the roof can seem dark and dull, but with the slightest break in the clouds the station interior comes alive with light. Calatrava's Lyon Satolas has the rare and supreme quality of looking beautiful even on the grimmest days with the flattest light.

Today's fashionable High Tech palette consists largely of shades of grey. In the hands of a master like Sir Norman Foster, who studies and calculates every angle and gradation of light, cool colours can be infinitely subtle and satisfying. Similarly Seville's Santa Justa, built of pale brick without, is all soft whites within. But strong colour has a role to play and Grimshaw uses bright blue steel work to brilliant effect at Waterloo. The colour is perfectly chosen to match the intense luminous blue of the sky on a clear day, and when the light catches the downward tapering stems of the trusses, highlighting them against the solid panels of the roof, the station can look like a cavern of blue stalactites.

These effects of changing light are one of the most fascinating aspects of new stations. Grimshaw's all glass outer wall at Waterloo, precisely because of its rippling curves, creates the kind of dappled reflections and shadows associated with light reflected on water. Calatrava makes brilliant play with shadows in the pergolas he has created above Stadelhofen Station in Zurich. Here the shadows of the steelwork fall on distinctly indented concrete panels creating a pattern like that of pennants rustling in the wind.

Reijnders and Kilsdonk and their colleagues have gone a stage further in bringing bright colour to town and suburban stations. Many railway lines in Holland are built on high embankments which provide good views but are very exposed to driving winds from the North Sea. Observation showed the Netherlands Railway architects how much people enjoy the sun, yet wish to escape the wind. Holland's new stations, in whole or part, are like conservatories, pleasant and protected places to stand or sit and wait.

Dutch railway architects are very concerned about their rating on the social security scale – the actual and perceived safety of passengers, especially at night. For this reason, new Dutch stations are designed to be as open as possible, with views across platforms and vertically between passenger concourses. Waiting rooms are brightly lit glass boxes, resembling gold fish bowls, where every movement can be seen by station staff and other passengers.

Reijnders' new station at Rotterdam Blaak takes night-time illumination to a new peak for a public building. Here is as much colour and novelty of form as the stage at a major pop concert. Brightly lit escalators and stairs add a thrill to the descent to the platforms: at any time of day there are always passers-by simply gazing into the great space below. The platforms are brought alive by brightly coloured tiles – all fresh strong yellows, reds, blues and blacks. The really eye-catching features, however, are the plant rooms, enclosed in standard clear glass bricks. Simply by placing blue lamps behind, Reijnders has created pools of light as intense and luminous as the sea on a Caribbean beach.

The key to the design of the new generation of train sheds is the adventurous use of structural steel. At Waterloo, individual components were honed and sculpted to perfection, with the help of full-size drawings and models in wood, plastic and wax. The steel used at Waterloo is tubular, but many of the tubes are tapering which meant they had to be manufactured specially. In the process, however, they were physically tested, allowing a great refinement of dimensions and thereby elegance of form.

While most structural engineers tend to specialise in either steel or concrete, Peter Rice was equally adept at both. His roof at Roissy is an accomplished symphony in tubular steel and visually, a modern day counterpart of the Forth Railway Bridge.

Rice and Hunt give such sculptural pliability to steel. Calatrava, like Rice, is masterful with both steel and concrete. His steel canopies at Stadelhofen bring a novel sinewy elegance to the elementary forms of both column and beam. Calatrava is also a master of elegance and line. This stems from the fact that many of his designs originate in free-hand sketches. He draws curves with the confidence of an artist. Picking up a piece of paper, he will explain one of his schemes with rapid sketches. He draws the particular curves of the structure with the ease and assurance with which most people sign their names.

Calatrava's greatest achievement is to impart a new poetry, and suppleness, to concrete. Most of the exciting new train sheds illustrated in this book are in steel and glass. Calatrava's Lyon Satolas is the exception, and to my mind it is as remarkable as any. He can shape concrete as intriguingly and crisply as if it were origami. His interlacing vaults have the verve of the early eighteenth-century Baroque-Gothic of Santini in Moravia. He says:

Concrete, to me, is probably the most noble construction material there is. My interest is centred on introducing a new vocabulary, of soft forms of a surrealist character, in tune with the spirit of the times.

Calatrava has led the way to more organic form. With it comes the revival of Expressionism in architecture

– a movement that seemed to die with Eric Mendelsohn in the 1930s, but now emerges with new possibilities thanks to today's technological advances. Grimshaw, interestingly, uses the word organic to describe the snaking roof of his new Waterloo terminal. Contrasting his approach with that of Sir Norman Foster he says, 'He is more like Mies, interested in geometric perfection. I prefer organic forms'.

There is an interesting sculptural element in the buffers at Waterloo. These are smooth, abstract, concrete ramps and contrast with the parallel descending ramps he has designed for the trolleys bringing food up to the Eurostar trains. All the engineers and architects who have created the new station architecture would emphasise the strongly functional character of their work. Functionalism, at least in the mind of the public, is associated with anonymous concrete or glass boxes. The genius of the new station architecture is to make the structural form expressive, adventurous and elegant. John Ruskin, the great critic of revivalist styles in railway stations, would have approved:

> . . . better [to] bury gold in the embankments than put it in ornaments on the stations. Railway architecture has, or would have a dignity of its own, if only it were left to its work. You would not put rings on the fingers of a smith at his anvil.

It is the willingness to go beyond the basic RSJ or I-beam that is the making of the new railway stations. However it is the Dutch who have gone furthest in using symbolism and eye-catching motifs to add joy to their stations. As Reijnders says, 'You know the old saying "Less is more". Well, we say less is a bore'.

Two factors make a railway station distinct from any other building, most notably from an airport terminal. Firstly, its position as a focal point, usually in the centre of a town, but also in suburban neighbourhoods. For this reason most stations need to be eye-catching, to proclaim unmistakably what they are. In a busy street it can be all too easy to miss a turning. Farrell's new station at Kowloon will be particularly striking in this way. The pedestrian entrances are in the flanks of a spectacular central arch, while the vehicle entrances have dramatic canopies sweeping out over four lanes of traffic.

Secondly, for all the new automation – and the need in many cases for fewer ticket offices – the station concourse has again become a focal point. From the Railway's point of view it is an opportunity to raise revenue from station traders – newsagents, cafes, restaurants – and to make the station more of a focal point in city life. It is the Spanish, above all, who have made the most of their concourses. In Atocha Station in Madrid, Rafael Moneo has created

an astonishing palm house in the old 1892 train shed. In Seville, the Santa Justa Station by Antonio Cruz and Antonio Ortiz astounds with the grandeur of its interior spaces.

The climax of any major railway station is, or should be, the train shed. Here is the opportunity to create vast covered spaces, the more breathtaking often because they are unsupported by any internal columns. The great train shed at St Pancras, by the engineer William Barlow, remained the largest for nearly a century. Interestingly the preference in Britain for column-free spaces, by contrast with, say, the Gare du Nord in Paris, had its origin in experience. A train had crashed into a column at the Bricklayers' Arms station, and brought down a large part of the roof.

Anthony Hunt explains light-heartedly that it was the experience of banging his head as a child when not looking where he was going which led him to persuade British Rail to dispense with the masts and wires roof they had envisaged initially for Waterloo.

Peter Rice's interest in transparency led him to experiment in a different way. To create pure walls of glass from track bed to roof, uninterrupted by columns, he supported his great trusses at Roissy internally, using pairs of giant pylons, spreading out like huge fingers to take the weight of the 'croissant' trusses.

With such large areas of brightly coloured steel and clear glass it is vital that the new generation of stations is kept sparklingly clean. External steel work will be washed and dried by rain and wind to some extent, but soot can accumulate in crevices and corners, particularly those out of the prevailing wind. Much more serious is internal steel work, especially if it is brightly coloured. Over several months a coating of dust will accumulate on top of steel trusses and ties and any feeling of smartness or freshness is from then on dispelled. Dutch Railways has learnt this lesson most effectively. At Sloterdijk, Reijnders introduced permanent gantries, in the form of ladders on rails, which slide along the outside of the glass tunnels enclosing the upper tracks. The result is that the station remains as new. Grimshaw, who is equally conscious of the need to keep glass clean, tackles the problem in a different way, using abseilers or cherry pickers – vehicles with mobile platforms such as those used to change bulbs in lampposts.

The key is to give the public a proper opportunity to appreciate these spectacular spaces, their beauty in changing light and their different character by day and night. Interestingly, this subject raised a great deal of debate a century ago. Baedekers' guide of 1907 to *Paris and Environs* complains of the Paris stations: 'Before starting, travellers are generally cooped up in the close and dusty waiting rooms, and are not admitted to the platforms until the train is ready to receive them'.

In the United States passengers also waited inside the main station building rather than on the platform. But as E B Ivatt, goods manager of the Midland Great Western Railway, commented in his *Railway Management of Stations* (I quote from the fourth edition of 1904), 'The British biped likes to meander up and down a railway platform [and] would raise a loud outcry if curtailed of his present liberty to do so'.

With the new Channel Tunnel trains, there is a move towards holding passengers in airport-style departure lounges. So it is vital that the architects designing these spectacular new train sheds, ensure they are open to public view as much as possible. Grimshaw achieves this at Waterloo by leaving the buffer end of his train shed completely open. Any user of Waterloo Station can see the striking new Eurostar trains as they pass through the concourse.

Moneo, in Madrid, provides a spectacular view into his new train shed at Atocha Station from the upper level where cars and taxis come into the station. Lille-Europe is conceived almost like a terraced hillside, with one level looking down to the next. Calatrava, in Lyon, has placed the tracks for the non-stopping trains in a concrete box running down the middle of the station. On top, is a spacious promenade for passengers to stretch their legs, and enjoy the building. From the upper level you have a much closer view of the remarkable ribbed vaults – rather like viewing a cathedral roof from the upper arcade or triforium.

High-quality architecture depends in considerable part on competitiveness and the existence of variety and choice. Though High Tech is the style of the moment, with its transparency and emphasis on daring spans, it is significant that the new generation of stations varies from minimalist to monumental, from cool Neo-Modernism with an emphasis on horizontals and right angles, to highly sculptural and organic buildings.

This book concentrates on stations which have been, or will soon be completed. Inevitably there are some spectacular projects which have been passed over in favour of rival schemes. On the grand scale, the most remarkable was Sir Norman Foster's scheme for a new through station beneath St Pancras and King's Cross in London, allowing Channel Tunnel trains to continue on through London to the rest of Britain.

Although much of the station was underground it had a spectacular glass-walled concourse that would successfully have held its own between two acknowledged masterpieces of railway architecture. In plan it was a simple sharp triangle – a little more pointed than a pennant flag. The roof was subdivided into nine further triangles arranged in a 1,3,5 pattern. The spaces between each billowing section of roof were filled with clear glass and the whole structure was held aloft on nine slender columns resembling the shape of baseball bats. Walls consisted of huge sheets of glass with slender inobtrusive supports. Subsequently, the British Government decided on a new scheme, with the Eurostar trains arriving above ground in the old St Pancras terminal, but Foster's roof will remain an icon.

The latest railway architecture demonstrates the key role stations have in town planning. 'The environs of most major railway stations in Europe are pretty grim', wrote George Millar in his classic war escape story *Horned Pigeon*. In the nineteenth century, stations produced gusts of soot and smut and were never fashionable neighbourhoods. Most stations of any size were also surrounded by large goods yards which kept antisocial hours and generated a continuous stream of heavy traffic. Today these goods yards have closed and most trains are electric, producing far less pollution than motor traffic. Stations and the precincts around them can be clean, pleasant and urbane.

In Holland, municipalities regularly contribute to improvements around stations. At Lelystad a large station piazza has been specially paved – not just the pedestrian areas, but the roads, cycle ways and bus stops. In Hong Kong, Terry Farrell's new station at Kowloon is the centrepiece of a whole new city district with over one million square metres of shops, offices, hotels and housing, including some four thousand flats.

WATERLOO INTERNATIONAL TERMINAL

WATERLOO STATION, LONDON

Architects: *Nicholas Grimshaw and Partners;* Structural Engineers: *YRM Anthony Hunt & Partners (roofing and glazing)*
Commissioned: *1988;* Construction: *1990–93*

The new Waterloo is a triumph of High Tech – an engineering and architectural solution of great beauty and ingenuity that is a direct response to an extraordinarily difficult site.

According to Nicholas Grimshaw the new terminus took one thousand man years to design. 'Like a Gothic cathedral the station is made up of relatively few components infinitely refined.'

The form of the new terminal is substantially determined by the alignment of the existing tracks and the site boundary on the west. This was the only space available in what is one of London's busiest commuter stations. But while the existing platforms were built for trains of no more than twelve conventional coaches, the new Eurostar passenger trains serving the Channel Tunnel were to be 400 metres in length. Tony Hunt, the engineer, recalls:

> When I was first called in by British Rail I was shown a model. It was a masts and wires solution by BR's own architects, with no engineering input. When asked to comment I said it was too elaborate, there were too many columns and too many cables.

Anthony Hunt Associates was formally asked to do a feasibility study on the design of a new roof in March 1987. The new terminal had to have a completely self-contained existence. In character it resembles an airport more than a conventional station, containing immigration and customs points, arrival and departure lounges, as well as the usual ticket hall.

Grimshaw resolved this by creating the new terminal on four levels. The upper level – the platforms – is on the same level as the existing tracks; one level below are the departure lounges; below that, the arrivals and finally the car parking.

At the lower levels the new terminal makes substantial use of the railway arches and vaults beneath the existing station and there are also facilities for staff and management.

The exciting part, nonetheless, is the long train shed, although Grimshaw emphasises it represents only ten per cent of the cost. Like Hunt, Grimshaw freely acknowledges inspiration from the great train sheds of the past:

> We were intensely aware of the great structures of earlier termini – from York to Leipzig. It's a type of building that invites excitement and the sense of getting up and going.

The train shed therefore is the wholly visible part of the building. There is no attempt to disguise or screen it – Grimshaw desires that it should proclaim its purpose and looks forward to the day when the buildings along York Road (which largely hide the new station) are demolished, exposing the full flank to view. His early drawings show the present York Road offices regrouped as two towers at either end of the train shed.

Huge glass sides descending to the level of the tracks all around the station make it a brightly lit beacon at night, serving as its own advertisement.

One key problem was to resolve how the mouth of the train shed, at the buffer end, should meet the rest of the building. While the existing Waterloo station is laid out on a grid with straight tracks, the concourse wrapped around the platform ends follows a gradual curve which is more pronounced where the new terminal is situated.

Grimshaw and BR were both concerned that the new trains should be visible from the concourse, communicating to every passenger the excitement and immediacy of the new direct link with France.

The solution is brilliant. The mouth of the new station is simply left open like a great proscenium arch. The theatrical effect is further emphasised by the new ticket area below the existing concourse, which creates the feeling of being in the front row of the stalls viewing the stage across the orchestra pit. The lower ticket level also makes a Channel Tunnel departure into a distinct event with its own sleek escalators taking passengers away from the rush hour throng above.

The other feature that catches the eye is the asymmetry: the curve of the roof is much steeper on one side than the other. The explanation is simple, there are five tracks not four, so that on one side the roof can rise gradually over a platform while on the other it must rise more sharply to clear the train. 'To avoid the train banging its head,' explains Hunt,

'It took us six months to work out a universal structural

system for the whole roof', states Grimshaw. The organic form, looking from the air like a well fed python, was finally resolved into four distinct sections. First is a straight section, second is a curving or radial section of the same span, third is a 'reducing section' in which the dimension of the arches steadily diminishes; and the fourth is another straight section. Grimshaw continues:

> The twisting nature of the structure would have made a standard glazing system extraordinarily expensive, involving thousands of different sizes and shaped components. To overcome this a loose-fit approach was adopted, in which a limited number of different-sized panes are used, each held in its own frame, and overlapping at the top and bottom like roof tiles.

The arched roof is in two distinct parts – a steeply rising transparent glass wall on the outer flank, giving a view across the river as the trains roll into the station, and a more complex ridged roof on the inner side, where glass alternates with solid panels. The clear glass wall covers one third of the span, the ridged roof the other two-thirds.

The structural principle of the roof is thus an arch made of two trusses, a major and a minor one, pinned together at the top. Hunt explains, 'the trusses are joined with cast steel knuckles and stainless steel pins. A similar connection is made at the base where the trusses almost sit on the platforms'.

The very different character of the two sides of the roof also results from the fact that the longer 'major' truss is inside the roof, and the shorter 'minor' above it. Both trusses are of distinctive bowstring form and banana shape. According to Hunt, the bowstring form is necessary to accommodate the bending created by uneven load conditions, and the building's shape.

Much of the High Tech character of the roof comes from the slenderness and lightness of the tubes forming the trusses. Andrew Whalley, the associate in charge of the project, explains how they wanted a tapered tube which couldn't be bought off the shelf; each element had to be tapered individually: 'We visit factories regularly. Here we did physical testing as well as standard engineering calculations. We were testing a prototype structure with sandbags hanging off it'.

Illustrations supplied by the practice show the extreme care that went into the design of each component. 'We went for steel sandcasting. We would do freehand sketches, then we made full-size models of many components. The actual castings were made by the lost wax process – a ceramic mould would be formed round a wax model, as it heated the wax would melt leaving the mould for the metal to be poured in.'

The massive weight of the long trains creates strong waves of pressure as they roll into the station, particularly when braking. The glazing system was therefore designed to compensate for this, by allowing the individual sheets of glass to overlap without actually touching. As Hunt reveals:

> The gaps between the glass are sealed vertically with an accordion style gasket and horizontally by a wiper blade. Together these seals allow standard square panels of glass to be fitted to the varied steel geometry like the skin of a snake or an armadillo.

The project architect, Neven Sidor, describes the practical pressures:

> When we started in 1988, we were presented with five tracks and a railway timetable. BR wanted provision for two trains arriving within five minutes of each other, each with up to seven hundred and fifty passengers. Fifteen minutes later the same trains have to leave.
>
> There are computer models available for airport and railway terminal design. They analyse the bottlenecks – at passport control, customs, security checks and ticket inspection – and give you the separation that must be provided between them.

He defines the building as a pump for people. As space is tight, it is designed to function alternately in departure and arrival modes, using the same staircases, escalators and lifts. The emphasis everywhere is on free flow and ease of movement. The ticket hall has a continuous open counter like a travel agent, rather than the usual glass fronted booths. Inside the lounges, the seats are plentiful, but never interrupt the passage of anyone wishing to walk straight through.

Concealing services posed a particular challenge. The solution was to set them into sloping panels in the ceiling, rather like the overhead lockers in an aeroplane, which flip open at any point to allow access for maintenance.

The architects' one regret is that they were not allowed to set glass pavement lights into the platforms and so bring daylight down to the departure lounges. On a sunny day, however, it means that the station's remarkable steel and glass roof comes as a pleasurable surprise. While the departure lounges – like many of today's high-tech interiors – are predominantly in shades of grey, Grimshaw's station roof is dominated by the brilliant cornflower blue of the steel work. With a blue sky above you might already be in the Mediterranean.

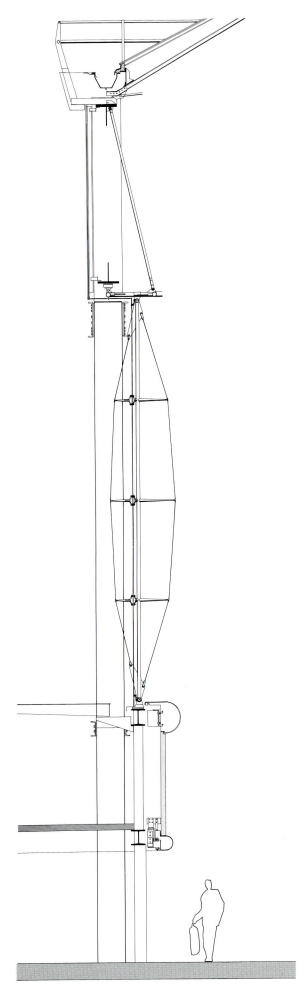

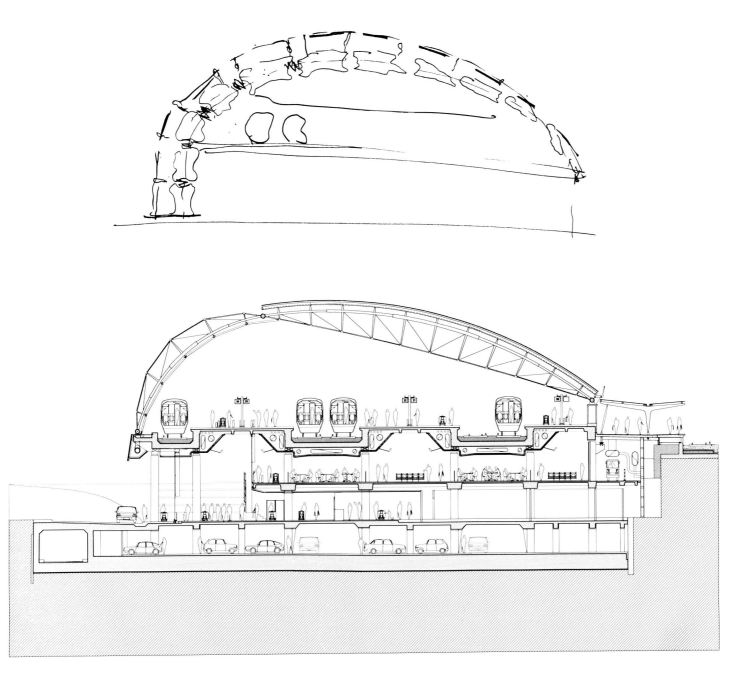

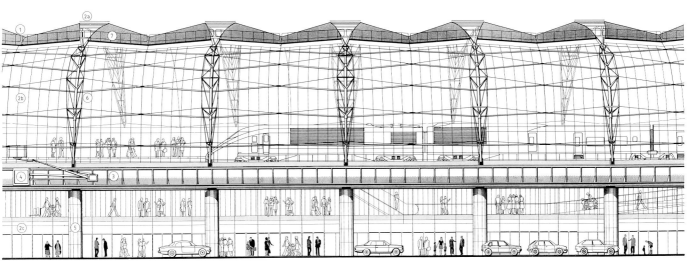

OPPOSITE LEFT: Section through bow string glass wall; FROM ABOVE: Concept sketch; cross-section through departure and arrivals halls; detail of front elevation

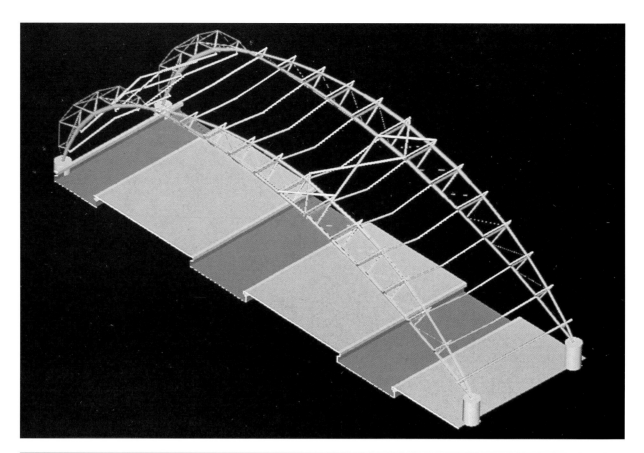

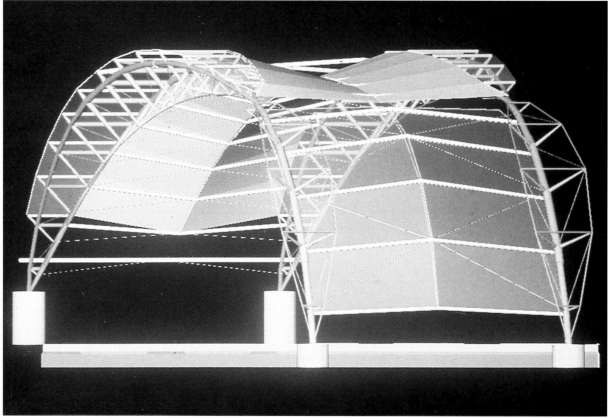

FROM ABOVE: Computer model of roof bay structure; computer model of cladding and glazing systems on roof bay
OPPOSITE, FROM ABOVE: Roof plan; arrival level plan;departure level plan

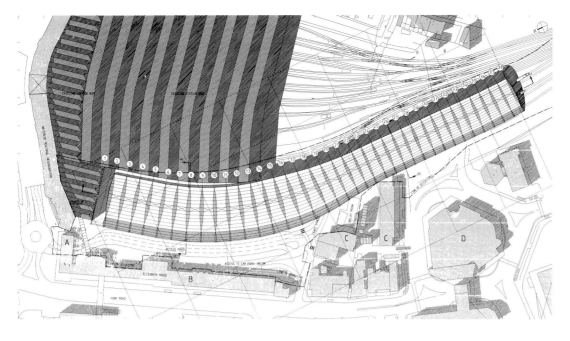

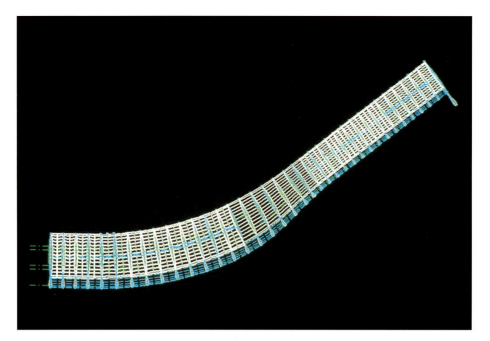

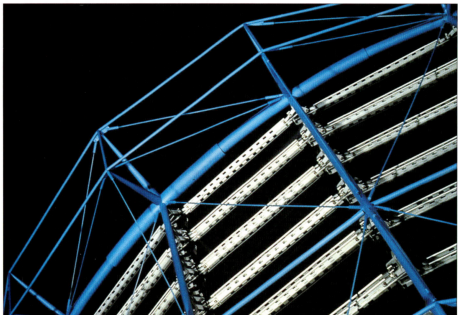

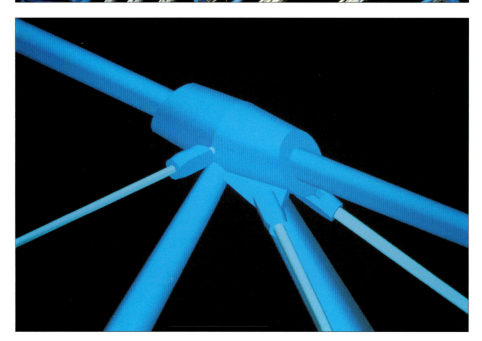

ABOVE: Computer generated structure plan; CENTRE and BELOW: Computer model of roof structure

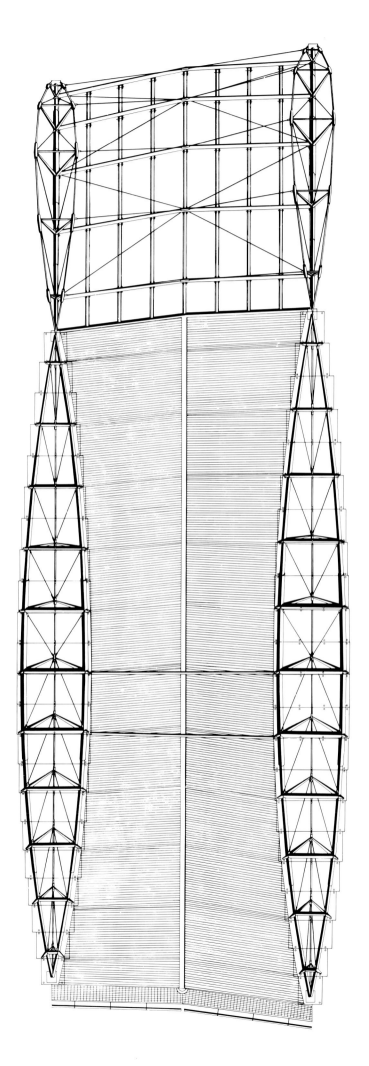

Plan of roof bay

ROISSY
Roissy-Charles De Gaulle Airport, Paris, France

Architects: *Paul Andreu, Chief Architect of Aéroports de Paris, and Jean-Marie Duthilleul, Chief Architect of French Railways; Engineer: Peter Rice with RFR; Start of design: 1989; Construction: 1991–94*

The Sun King, Louis XIV, would surely have approved of the plan of the new TGV station at Roissy. The whole layout of station and air terminals with its grand axis, rigid geometry and absolute symmetry makes the complex the Versailles of airport design.

Initially, the plan was to place the new station midway between Terminals 1 and 2, but for Paul Andreu, Chief Architect of Aéroports de Paris, there was only one place for the station to go: exactly between the existing Terminal 2 and the planned Terminal 3. This way the new station would be at the hub of the airport in the next century, with railway and road intersecting at precise right angles.

Andreu's original cylindrical Aérogare 1 remains one of the most remarkable of all airport terminals, with its circular courtyard criss-crossed by flying escalators. His Terminal 2, or rather, Terminals 2A, 2B, 2C and 2D have grown on a different principle. Each is on a banana-shaped plan, the aim of which is to cut sprint distance from car or taxi to plane to the very minimum. According to Andreu, one does not need not walk more than 50 metres to the departure gate.

The new station, which opened in November 1994, has six platforms, four for the TGV and two for the RER, the fast trains which connect Roissy with the centre of Paris. The TGV trains, by contrast, are on a line which bypasses Paris, connecting with Lille and the Channel Tunnel to the north, and Lyon to the south.

The new tracks are naturally set below ground so that they pass beneath the runways. Two island platforms, each 490 metres long, serve the TGV trains, with two through tracks for high-speed trains in the centre. The two RER tracks are served by shorter, 275 metre platforms. At ground level the main hall contains all SNCF station services; the ticket offices, telephones, news stands and refreshments.

A mezzanine level above provides access to an airport shuttle train service offering a fast link to all the airport terminals. The fourth level, equipped with travelators, provides pedestrian links to Terminal 2 and to Terminal 3, if and when it is built, as well as to parking areas. Lastly, the fifth level opens on to the road, and a set down for cars, taxis and coaches. In 1997 the antici-

pated passenger traffic for the station is 1.7 million, rising to 2.5 million in the long term.

The design of the station is a cooperative effort by Paul Andreu, Jean-Marie Duthilleul, Chief Architect of French Railways and the late Peter Rice, widely regarded as the greatest structural engineer of his age.

Given a very free hand by Andreu and Duthilleul, Rice's design for the station roof in particular, can be seen as one of the purest expressions of engineering genius and invention of our time. Unmistakably in this case, the engineer was responsible primarily for the whole concept and refinement of the structure. Andreu explains:

> Our aim was to write something new in the tradition of glass and steel. The question we asked ourselves was what would nineteenth-century people do with our means.

> High Tech architecture tends to give you a lesson in structure. What concerned us most was the quality of light. The aim was to let light flood down onto the tracks. We wanted to avoid the deep dark of the night which comes with clear glass overhead. So instead, we chose translucent glass which remains white in the evening.

The roof is in four sections rising towards a new six-storey Sheraton Hotel, set above the centre of the station. The outer two sections are level but gently arched. The inner two rise steeply towards the hotel, flattening out as they reach the top.

The great beauty of the station is undoubtedly the interior; a temple to the art of structural engineering. Not since the Forth Bridge has tubular structure achieved such poetry and complex rhythm. Just as the Forth Bridge presents a constantly changing web of intersecting steel tubes, first coming closer then retreating, so Rice's forest of white steel – vertical, diagonal and bowed – is seen in constantly changing perspectives as you move around the station. It has a kaleidoscopic fascination, challenging you to shoot off reels of film in the search for the perfect viewpoint.

From below the effect is akin to the rigging of a great sailing ship. It only needs the ship's company to scale the masts, run out along the booms and salute the admiral as he reviews the fleet.

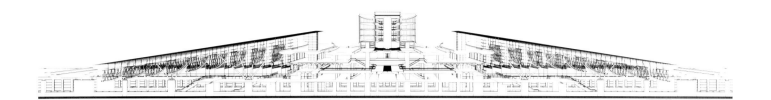

Rice offers you the opportunity of gazing in wonder at the sheer bravura of it all, or working out, step by step, why the whole gigantic structure has not come crashing down on your head. The game, of course, is to carry the maximum expanse of roof on the minimum number of internal supports without any weight resting on the all glass walls.

Station roofs traditionally arch upwards. Rice, as if defying gravity, turns his trusses upside down, so their size and weight is all the more apparent. The beauty lies in the way they are stepped one above the next, raising the roof ever higher, so that whether you are at the top or the bottom you constantly see the whole series, each framing the other. Rice called them 'croissant' beams, describing them as having 'a strong curved double bottom boom and a thin tensile top chord'. They are supported on sturdy fan-shaped pylons set on concrete piers. Moreover, the lower pylons have two arms, the second three and the third four.

To add to the complexity there is not one vertical column in the place and the arms of the pylons are all diagonals. Although there are two rows of pylons, each supporting the trusses at two points, the support for each truss comes only from one side. Above, longitudinal and transverse bracing combine with the pylons to stabilise the structure.

Both the glass for the roof and the side walls is fixed directly to the steelwork. Hugh Dutton, the project leader at RFR describes their approach:

The concept is quite different from the way in which glass is usually fixed to steel using aluminium. Glass is very strong though brittle. Here, in the quest for transparency, its structural capacity has been exploited so as to dispense with the aluminium glazing bars, particularly on the side walls where a special articulated glass bolt protects the glass from local bending. On the roof the glass is laid directly on top of the steel grid, using the Fischer patented silicone gasket system.

Depending on the time of day and year, bright sunlight can flood in through the clear glass walls, or more filtered sunlight through the whiter glass of the roof. This also softens the shadows. The combination of white steel against white glass creates a powerful ethereal effect, more subtle than the strong chiaroscuro often created by clear glass and exposed structure. By night the effect is reversed. As Paul Andreu explains:

Internal uplighters play on the screen printed glass roof which filters and half-reflects, bathing the internal space in a slightly unreal light. Seen from outside, the lighted roof transforms the station into a magic lantern.

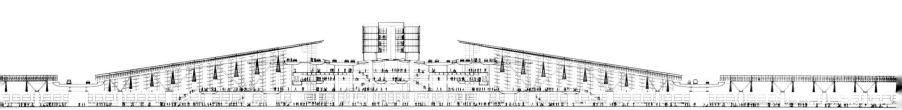

FROM ABOVE: Sectional perspective; longitudinal section

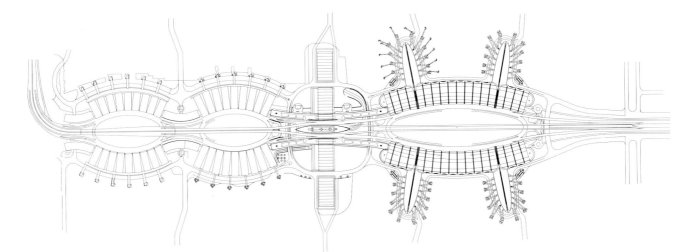

Site plan

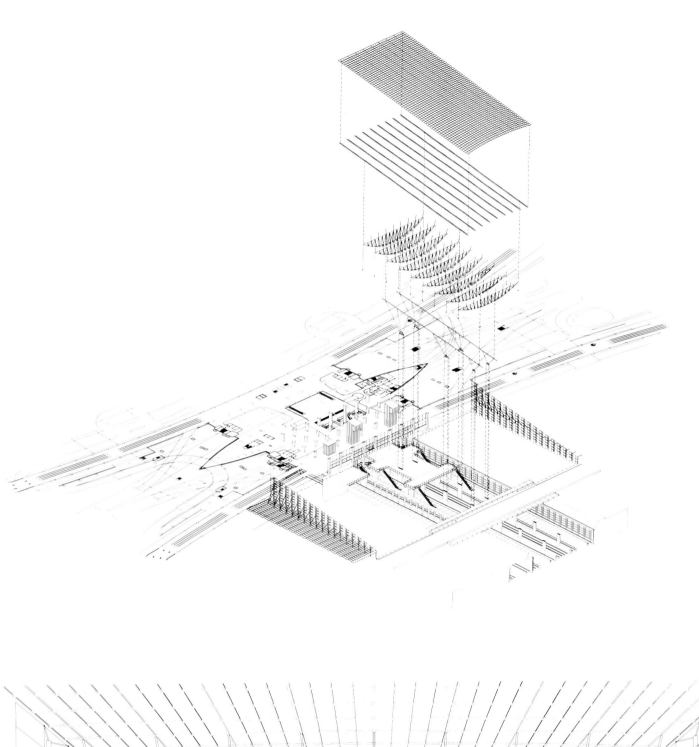

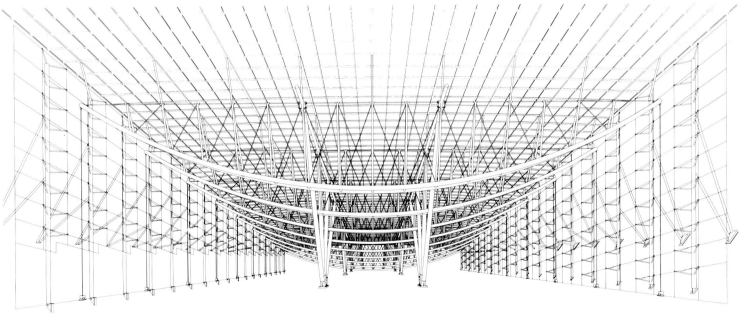

FROM ABOVE: Exploded isometric of the inclined glass roof; interior perspective of the inclined glass roof

LILLE-EUROPE

Lille, France

Architects: *Jean-Marie Duthilleul, Etienne Tricaud and Pierre Saboya;* Engineers: *Peter Rice with Jean-Francois Blassel of RFR and Sophie Lebourva of Ove Arup;* Start of design: *1988;* Construction: *1990–94*

Lille-Europe TGV station is a harbinger of the twenty-first century – the result of its floating magic carpet roof and the way in which it brings the new Channel trains into the heart of the city, forming the touchstone of a spectacular £620 million development.

'I'm not French,' stated Rem Koolhaas the Dutch architect who acted as master planner for the whole project, 'and I tell you, it's impressive to see how once a decision is taken in France, everything is mobilised to put it into effect'.

. . . the idea is simple. To modernise the city without destroying it. Nothing has been demolished to make way for the development. Lille was fortunate in having a large military area just outside the old city walls where by ancient edict no structure could be erected unless it could be dismantled in twenty-four hours.

When it came to choosing architects, Koolhaas adopted what he calls counter-typecasting:

Christian de Portzamparc had only designed major cultural buildings so we set him to work on an office block. Jean Nouvel has a reputation for expensive buildings so we gave him the challenge of designing a large shopping centre at a bargain price.

The decision to route the new TGV Nord–Europe line via Lille led to the decision to build a new through station. The old Lille–Flandres terminus 400 metres away could continue to serve the Paris–Lille TGVs while London and Brussels bound trains would use the new station.

At Lille-Europe station, the Chief Architect of SNCF, Jean-Marie Duthilleul gave his engineer, Peter Rice, the brief of recapturing the spirit of great nineteenth-century stations. The big difference is that while many Victorian stations were massively built, Lille-Europe is an essay in lightness of construction.

As at the former Gare d'Orsay in Paris, the tracks of the new station are set well below the main concourse level. Duthilleul describes it as 'a balcony station providing a view of the old city's skyline'. The three levels reflect the topography of the site. On the east side, an upper level deck connects with the road and pedestrian bridge over the passing expressway and

provides a drop off point for cars. Approaching from this side, you look down upon a cavernous underground hall, criss-crossed by escalators descending to the metro. This is called the Espace Piranesien and was designed by Rem Koolhaas.

Further on escalators lead down to the main concourse level which runs parallel with the tracks below, allowing a full view of the TGV platforms and trains. To the west, on the city centre side, a large square slopes down to the level of the tracks, allowing train passengers a panorama of the city. Escalators, lifts and staircases, located every 70 metres along the concourse provide access to trains. Numbers displayed over each access point allow passengers to use the access closest to the coach they will board.

The sense of openness and airiness is increased by the glazed walls which enclose the station on every side. These allow one to see the trains arriving and departing without entering the station.

The roof is supported by arches of surprising slenderness which proportionately look even slimmer than hula hoops. The effect is explained by Sophie Lebourva, the engineer at Ove Arup:

. . . this is a completely three-dimensional structure. Every member relies on its neighbours to be stable. The two main elements of structure are set at 90 degrees to each other – the arches and the cable beams. All structural elements are in one or other plane.

The roof does not rest directly on the arches but projects over small vertical posts rising from the arches. These posts do not touch the roof but carry the simple cable beam on which the roof actually rests. Even here the weight is not taken by a simple horizontal beam, but carried on a cross-brace, at the precise point where the ties cross. In many ways the structure seems closer to a high level trapeze than a traditional train shed roof. In construction terms, the use of arches enables the available support points to be exploited effectively. The arches are hollow steel tubes – not strict semicircles but made to two radii. The larger arch is 273 millimetres in diameter and has a span of 26 metres. The smaller arches have a diameter of

OPPOSITE: Schematic isometric view of roof bay structure

244 millimetres and a span of 18.5 metres. Small arches were brought to the site in one piece, the larger ones in two sections.

The arches are reinforced by steel ties which like the spokes of a wheel provide a safeguard against buckling. Peter Rice, his colleagues relate, used to say that people could be worried by ties but pointed out that they are safer than either columns or arches. 'It's reassuring to see a lot of matter and disquieting to see a little,' he used to say. As was his practice, he chose the unconventional option.

The design work on the roofing was carried out by RFR, the practice Peter Rice established in Paris. Jean-Francois Blassel explains their motive:

> We were aiming for lightness and immateriality. The initial scheme was for metal cladding discreetly punctured to let in light. But this would have revealed the thickness of the construction at the openings. So we worked towards a filter letting the light in but not allowing a view through. We sought an effect akin to clouds or the quality of light through foliage, bright not glaring.

Blassel considered that the roof could be a lightweight structure because '... there was nothing to put inside it, no services, no insulation'. He relates that there was also '... a strong demand from the acousticians for the roof to absorb sound and this precluded an all metal or all glass roof'. Thus they evolved a roof with a flat-bottomed V-shaped section which enabled the sound absorption to be increased artificially.

These V-sections contain all the geometric complexity of the roof – they do not touch but are joined by narrow strips of glass. Though the roof is not transparent it changes dramatically with the weather. When the light is flat or dull, it is quite opaque. However on a day when the sky is half overcast, and the sun suddenly comes out, the effect is magical; in Blassel's words, 'as if a giant lamp has been switched on'.

One of the most skilful aspects of the station design is the way it is integrated with the buildings and roads around it. Two office towers are actually built over the station roof with footings descending down on either side to create the desired impression of 'a magic carpet, floating under them'. At the same time the station roof is bisected by a high level road connecting the city centre with the suburb on the other side. As it crosses the new *place* in front of the station, the road is carried on one of the most elegant and minimalist of all modern bridges. The steel arches supporting the road deck are like infinitely slender crescent moons. They are not parallel to the road, but at right angles to it, conveying the same floating effect as the station roof. The bridge is by François Deslaugiers. Peter Rice could not have wished for a more brilliant response to his search for lightness of form.

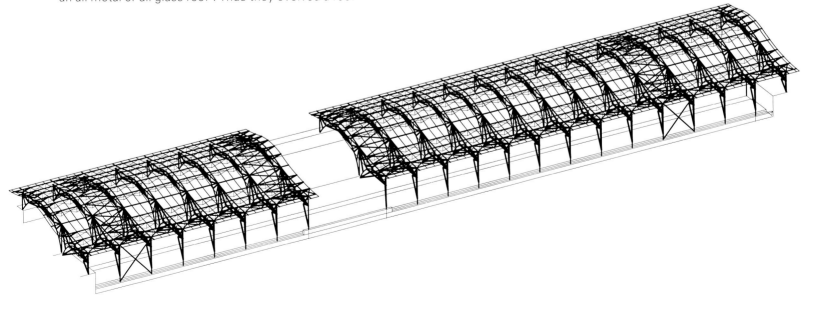

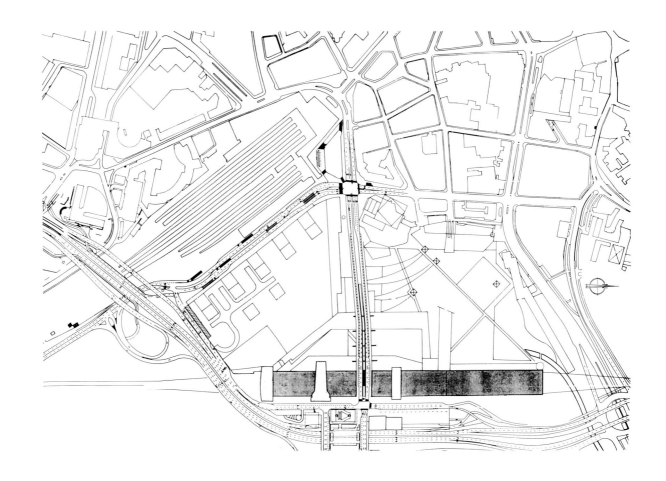

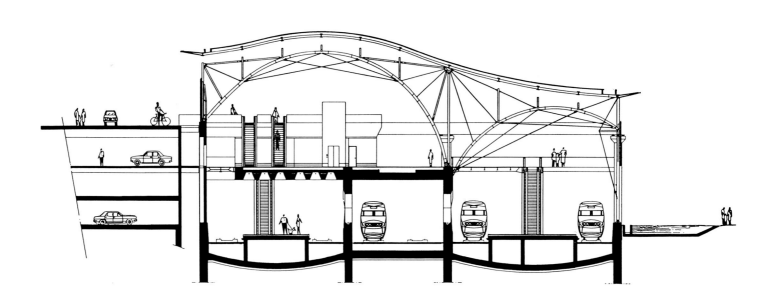

OPPOSITE, FROM ABOVE: Elevation of end wall; site plan; cross section showing arrival and departure areas

OPPOSITE, FROM ABOVE: Typical section through canopy structure; east elevation; west elevation

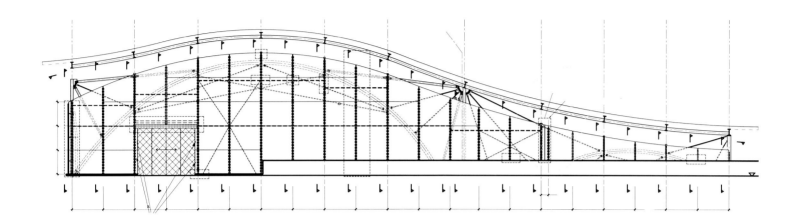

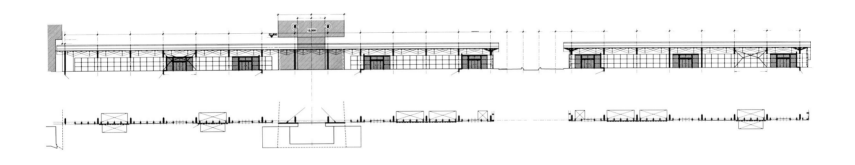

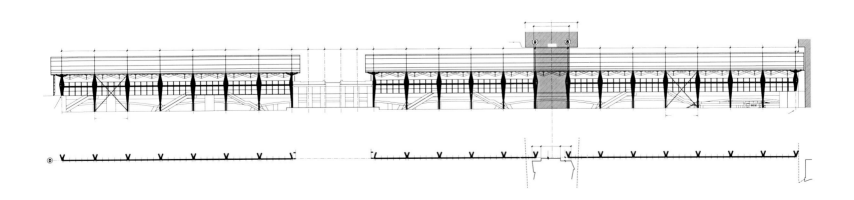

LYON SATOLAS
LYON, FRANCE

Architect and Engineer: *Santiago Calatrava;* Construction: *1989–94*

Calatrava's new station at Lyon Airport is, for me, a building worth travelling half way round the globe to see. Here the Expressionist architecture of the early nineteenth century takes wings – architecture and sculpture are fused into a single art.

Like many great monuments Lyon Satolas station benefits from a certain isolation and loneliness. Approaching by road from Lyon you are in a landscape of huge flat fields. Suddenly you are conscious of a large deep cutting running parallel with the road – like a major shipping canal – where, in fact, the new TGV tracks lie just out of sight below.

Thanks to the staggering rhetorical gesture of *L'Oiseau* (the bird) the new station is by far the most commanding building of the whole airport site. Like many sculptural buildings it immediately suggests a whole range of analogies; a centurion's helmet, or from another angle, the crown of the Statue of Liberty.

Next the eye is seized by the long low train shed – with its shallow arc roof supported on an extraordinary web of concrete cross-frames. The road passes straight through the station, providing a sudden, dramatic glimpse of the tracks below and a perspective of arches – not conventional round or pointed arches – but Calatrava's characteristically tense and elongated vaults with outward sloping piers.

Almost simultaneously, there are mesmerising cross views, when for a fleeting moment all the structural elements line up, as in a cider orchard or quincunx.

In its design, the station has an almost superhuman element; its beauty lies in structural elements that are at once of enormous size and simplicity. Calatrava shapes concrete with the ease of origami; the plain smooth surfaces fold into clever and fascinating forms.

The Bird, as the central feature of the station, was conceived as a symbolic grand gesture proclaiming the marriage of high speed train and jet aeroplane at the gateway to the Alps. Anthony Tischauser of the Calatrava office states that it was clear from the brief that a monumental structure was desired, 'so Calatrava gave them this bird hovering above the tracks'. Some undoubtedly will see *L'Oiseau* as sheer self-indulgence, out of tune with today's revival of modernist simplicity.

Calatrava, however, responded not simply with an eye-catching exterior but with a stupendous interior space – as grand and memorable as any of the great North American passenger concourses.

The whole glass concourse hall roof rests on just three points; two huge steel arcs converge on a single point on the north side. These knuckles or nodules have the engineering power and simplicity of the footings of the Eiffel Tower while their sculptural quality is more apparent because they are set outside the envelope of the building.

Once inside the scale is breathtaking. There is the sense that every part of this building has its origin in forceful freehand drawing, rather than set square, ruler and compass. Instead of conventional vertical walls and flat roofs, every surface is on the slope, not in any gratuitous sense, but as if to add to the feeling of dynamic tension, of a structure built to contain vast forces. This is not megalomania, but an almost Renaissance sense of man stretching building techniques and materials to the limit.

The sense of sinew is apparent in the dramatic hairpin-shaped balconies protruding out over the interior, where even the seats are shaped like windsurf boards.

What makes *L'Oiseau* so appropriate as an airport station is the sense of streamlining, aerodynamics and equally, of attenuation. As well as curves, there is a web of dagger-shaped triangles created by the glazing and the flying ribs which support the projecting wings of the roof.

No less important for a glass house of this size, *L'Oiseau* is a supremely comfortable space in which to wait. In winter so large a space can never be fully heated but underfloor heating takes the chill out of the air. There are, surprisingly, no draughts and you can comfortably sit in an overcoat.

In summer, glass roof and walls might seem a recipe for stifling heat, but as the concourse is set above the platforms, Calatrava has been able to take brilliant advantage of a cool draught rising from the tracks below. At the press of a button the windows in the lower arc tilt automatically to allow in a pleasant rush of cooling air. This explains the unusually chunky detail

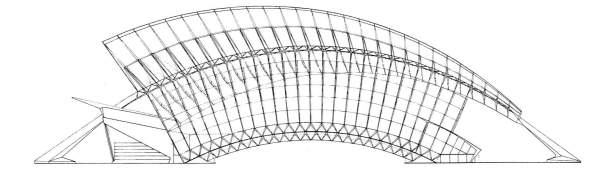

of the grips which hold the glass of these windows.

No less mesmerising are the views along the train sheds. Perfect symmetry reigns. There are six tracks and the two in the centre are contained in an enclosed concrete tunnel which allows TGVs to rush through the station at 300 kilometres per hour. Calatrava relishes the noise. 'It's like a volcano', he says; but the sound, although powerful, is not unpleasant.

The roof over the box tunnel serves as a promenade, or concourse, allowing passengers to walk freely in comfort to the escalator or elevator nearest to the point where their coach will stop. On either side there are impressive views down to the tracks, and the fact that the walls are open, not solid, increases the sense of airiness. What absorbs attention most of all is the roof – a web of ribs – seen in constantly changing combinations, like the interlaced vaults of late Gothic roofs such as the Wenceslas Hall in Prague Castle.

Much of the beauty comes from the fact that Calatrava's white concrete is as smooth as Roman travertine. The windows too, are powerfully made – almost like the port-holes of Captain Nemo's submarine, and as exotic in shape.

The cross-braces of the walls are another brilliant testament to Calatrava's artistic handling of mass. An early drawing suggests they were conceived as versions of Leonardo's famous man with outstretched arms inscribed in a square and circle. Calatrava's sketches imbue them with the sense of Atlas figures; their heads bowed against pressure. They also obey the engineering principle of downward forces tapering towards a narrow point.

One ultimate test of any great building is that it is photogenic from every angle. Wherever you move inside or outside, Lyon Satolas forms a fascinating and powerful picture for it was conceived completely in three-dimensions.

Brilliant too, is Calatrava's handling of light: the combination of white concrete and abundant roof lighting make it beautiful and cheering on a grey day. In a storm you are at once conscious of the elements and cocooned against them. On a blustery day with changing skies, the openness of the building and the numerous rooflights render a wonderful sense of moving clouds and sudden shafts of sun. In brilliant sunshine a positively Roman chiaroscuro is evoked.

Calatrava has characteristically incorporated his lighting within the structure, ensuring a minimum of furniture or gadgetry to disturb the bold simple forms. At night the illuminated glass roof makes the building a glittering landmark.

On the platforms below, there is an extraordinary array of furniture – seats, lamps, departure screens – perhaps too much for the simplicity of the building but which, in a strange way, peoples the platforms when they are empty.

The abiding thought this great station leaves is that Calatrava has a sense of natural rhythm exactly like that of a musician; many themes are repeated, but they are handled with supreme aplomb, composed so they are constantly seen in new and different combinations. Calatrava's magic infects even those who usually complain most about the teething problems of a building. 'C'est chef d'oeuvre' said the janitor, as he showed me the mechanism for the windows; a true compliment indeed.

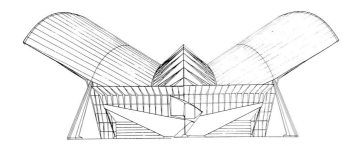

FROM ABOVE: North elevation; east elevation

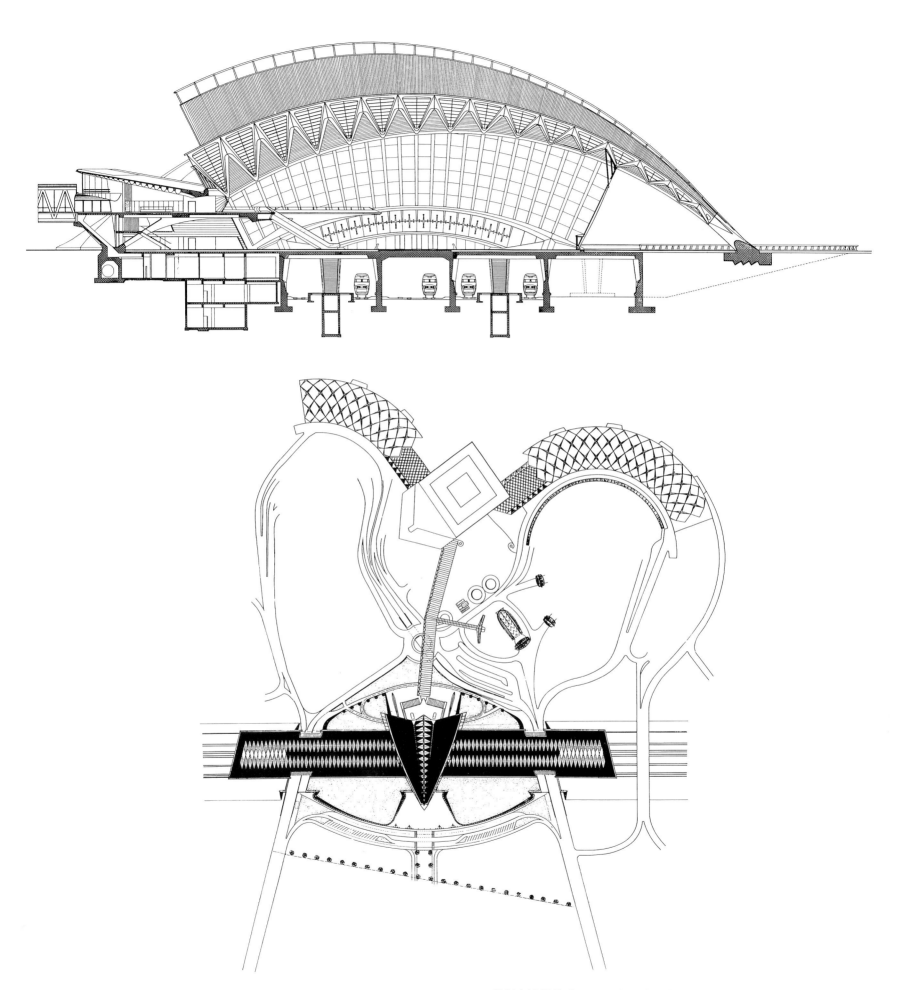

FROM ABOVE: Cross section; site plan

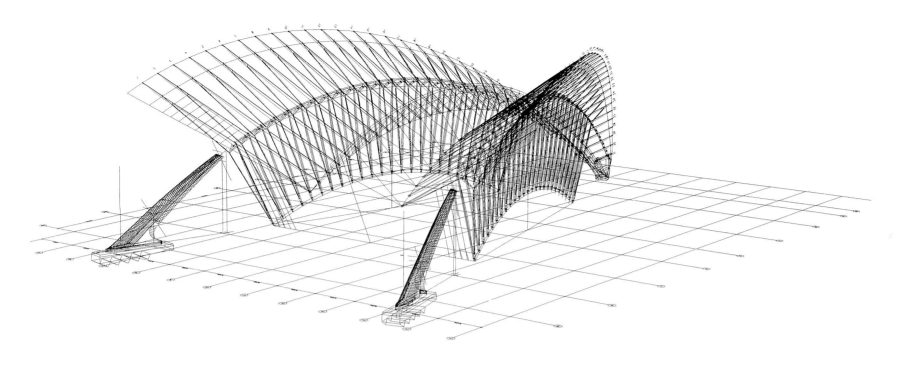

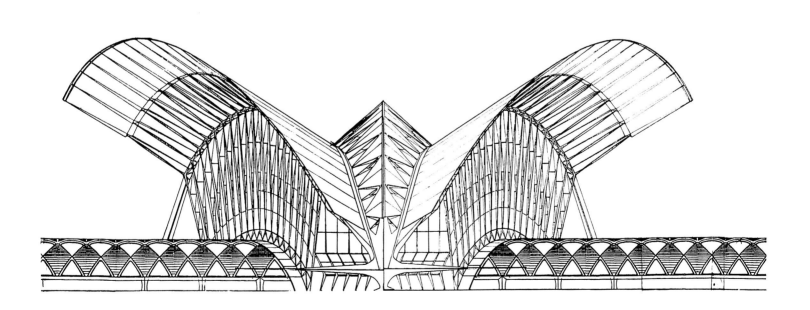

FROM ABOVE: Computer model of the structure of L'Oiseau; west elevation

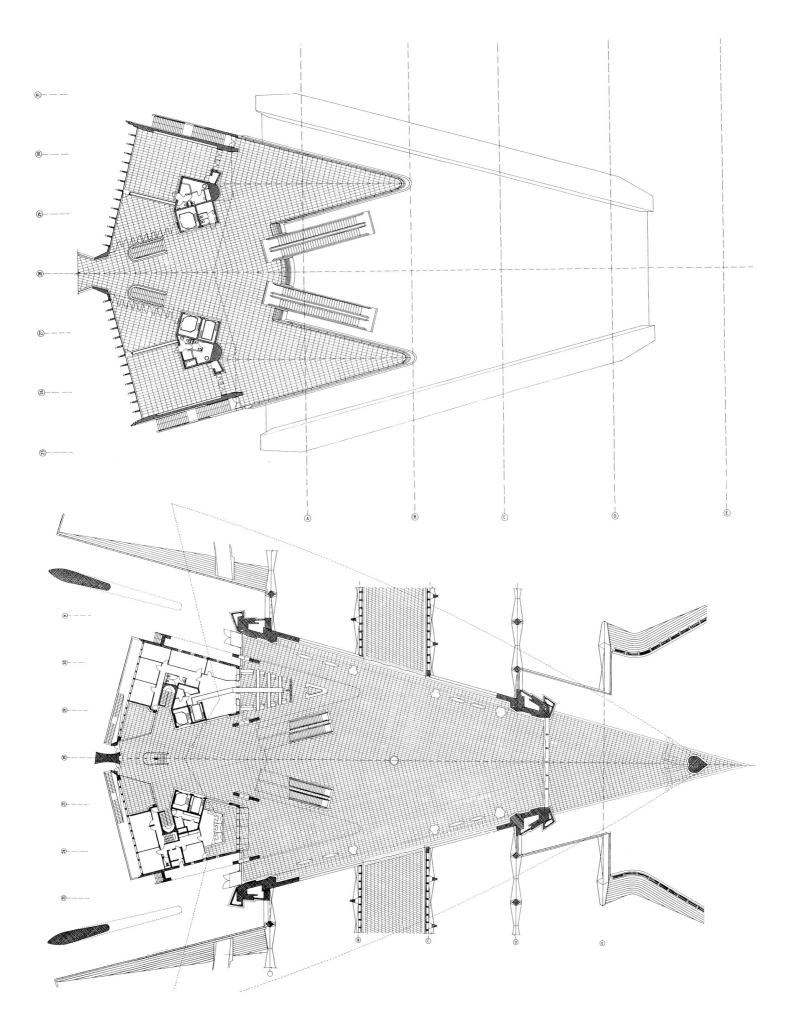

FROM ABOVE: Upper level plan; entry level plan

MARNE-LA-VALLÉE

EURODISNEY, MARNE-LA-VALLÉE-CHESSY, PARIS

Architect: *Jean-Marie Duthilleul, Etienne Tricaud, François Bonnefille;* Engineer: *Jean Pierre Coeur, Arcora;* Designed: *1988;* Construction: *1992–94*

This imposing station has its origins in the accord signed between the French state and the Disney Organization. Eurodisneyland was not only to have a major new station for the RER express to and from Paris but to be served directly by the new TGV line bypassing Paris to the East, connecting Lille directly with Lyon, and eventually northern Europe with Southern France.

Jean-Marie Duthilleul, chief architect of French railways, explains its role:

> It will be served by suburban trains and *Grandes Lignes*, both national and international, used by local commuters, businesses and holidaymakers. Ultimately it will help to tilt the balance of the Ile de France back towards the East.

The design of the station, continues Duthilleul, was:

> . . . the subject of long exchanges between Disney, including Michael Eisner in person, and the architects at SNCF. Our task was to express a real station in an artificial world – we had to re-invent the vocabulary we had evolved at Roissy and Lille.

The result was what he refers to as 'une facade de representation', a 'decorated wall three hundred metres long and a grand metallic hall plunging down to the platforms'.

The wall is nothing if not monumental, 300 metres long and 8 metres high, it is punctuated by five enormous arches – each large enough to span a sizeable river. It shelters not only the station (120 metres) but a large car park (180 metres). It is in blond concrete, with a red cornice emulating porphyry. As if to emphasise the separation of the two worlds, the wall is in fact a screen standing free from the station itself. Only on the glazed front overlooking the entrance to the Parc Disney does Duthilleul include a whimsical gesture – in the form of two candle-snuffer towers (rather like minarets) flanking the entrance.

The showpiece of the new station is the large central hall descending to the tracks, and surrounded by a promenade on two levels. The main level, opening onto the pavement outside has the SNCF and Eurodisney *services d'accueil* as well as shop and cafe. Above there is provision for further shops.

Everything is designed to show off the new TGV trains. Many visitors arrive by car and coach: walking into the station you see people looking down at the platforms, lining the balustrades to get a glimpse of what happens. Duthilleul knows that nothing attracts a crowd like a crowd.

Everything is rigidly symmetrical encouraging photographs to be taken along the central axis, but in fact the best views are the diagonal ones. From an angle, and viewed from the upper gallery the station hall is criss-crossed by almost as many bridges and stairs as one of Piranesi's *Carceri*.

The impression of an active environment is conveyed firstly by the escalators, four to each platform, two up and two down. The up and down escalators cross half-way and connect with a bridge across the middle of the hall. Nestling behind the escalators are staircases, turning at right angles to connect with the galleries at the side of the hall. At the ends further double staircases lead to the upper galleries, one of which is straight and one elegantly curved. Children could play games here for hours.

The sense of industry, akin to a railway workshop or steel foundry, is increased further by the roof, which is carried on a series of shallow inverted arches. At the level of the upper gallery you have the heightened effect of actually standing in the roof looking along avenues of suspended columns.

On platform level, the dramatic quality is achieved by the way in which the escalators form giant scissor motifs. Striding out along the 490-metre-long platforms the architecture becomes even more monumental. The concrete ceiling is deeply coffered, and the columns have capitals or tops like giant kitchen funnels, as if to emphasise the colossal weight they are supporting.

As on all the new TGV stations there is an astonishing array of black platform furniture. Its Dalek-like appearance seems entirely appropriate to the fantasy world in which you arrive.

Longitudinal section

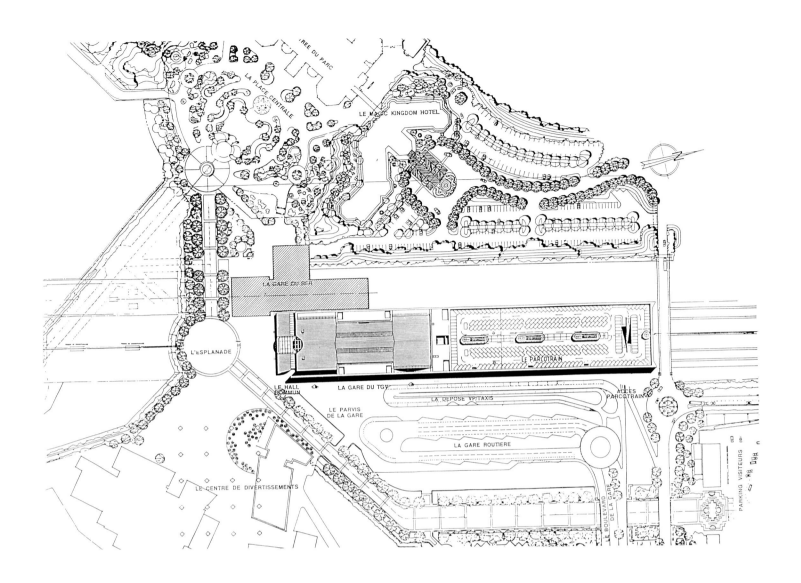

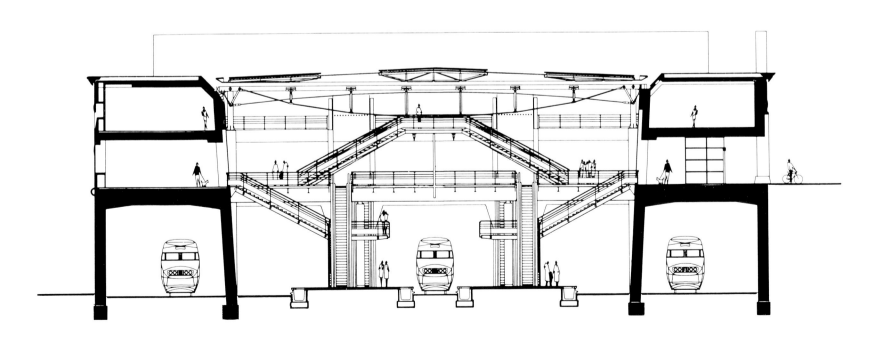

FROM ABOVE: Site plan; cross section

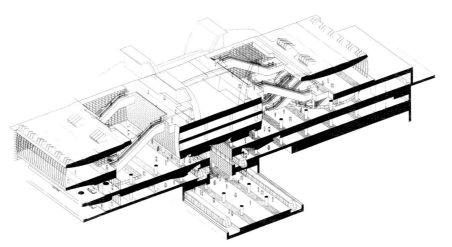

KOWLOON
HONG KONG

Architect: *Terry Farrell;* Engineer: *Ove Arup and Partners;* Designed: *1992;* Construction: *1994–97*

Farrell's new station at Kowloon is an epoch-making statement about public transport in the city of the future. The new station forms the centrepiece of a huge land reclamation of 17.3 hectares, laid out to a master plan by Farrell. Around the station will be four thousand five hundred flats, large quantities of offices, shopping and hotels – a total of one million square metres.

The new precinct will be laid out around three large landscaped squares surrounded by high-rise buildings. Vehicles will circulate around and beneath the development. The main level, artificially raised, will be largely pedestrian and free of traffic – though there will be drop off points for the individual buildings.

Farrell's new station is like an iceberg, with the larger part underground concealing its actual size. He explains the extent of its area:

> The station measures 300 metres by 180. You could fit Charing Cross station into a corner of the site. . . the best way to understand its sheer scale is from the taxi rank. There will be twenty simultaneous pick up points. If people were to take taxis one at a time as they do in London you'd never get the people off the trains.

Kowloon is on the line from Hong Kong Central to the new Airport at Chek Lap Kok, being built to the designs of Sir Norman Foster. 'The station will contain check-in counters for the airport – each train has a luggage coach', says Farrell. There are also two local lines.

The big change, however, will come when the border opens and all trains for the new airport will pass through Kowloon rather than Hong Kong Central. With 170,000 square metres it will be Hong Kong's biggest station. Farrell hesitates to put a precise cost on it, but settles on 'a figure in excess of £400 million'.

Above ground the station is simple and monumental. The gently arched roof, raised up on glass walls, is forcefully interrupted by four towers. The centre, between the towers, is open, forming a giant triumphal arch or gateway, providing shade for the station entrances. The form of these towers is slightly mysterious: it belongs neither quite to architecture nor to engineering. The deliberate avoidance of vertical lines smacks of buildings in space movies. There is also a certain sedateness in the curves – the kind of flattened curves found in American car design, and intended to convey comfort and reassurance. Farrell's sloping roofs have the feel of giant car bonnets. Roof cladding will be silver in colour. He explains: 'I like structures that are both solid and light'.

Concrete appeals to him because of its absolute certainty and sense of permanence. He has been critical of some of today's High Tech architecture. Contrary to appearances, he argues, 'much of the acrobatic steelwork you see is not structural but decorative.' He is also critical of transparency for its own sake, especially in office blocks. 'You create a hothouse and end up having to resort to immensely expensive measures to cool it down', he says, by way of explanation.

The place for transparency, in Farrell's view, is large concourses. Here, lofty spaces offer the possibility of natural ventilation. At Kowloon Farrell has introduced wells carrying light down three or even four storeys: 'We call them light chimneys', he states.

The road entrances are equally dramatic. Huge curving canopies sweep out over the road between two tower blocks. The canopies follow the gentlest of curves – like a length of cloth unfurled over an oriental doorway – and large sections of glass let light pour through.

Nearby Farrell has designed another highly sculptural building for the railway – the KVB – or Kowloon Ventilation Building. This provides the all important ventilation for the underground tracks and sits in a conspicuous position on the new waterfront. With its raised fins it has the look of a space craft or giant terrestrial vehicle from the science fiction world of Transformers. Brilliant colour – as yet not finalised – could make it one of the most eye-catching buildings on the waterfront. 'I like to give every building a personality', says Farrell.

OPPOSITE, FROM ABOVE: Axonometric section through station roof, concourse and rail tracks; site model; masterplan

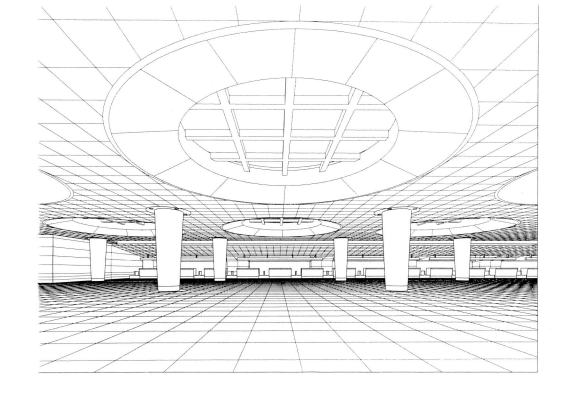

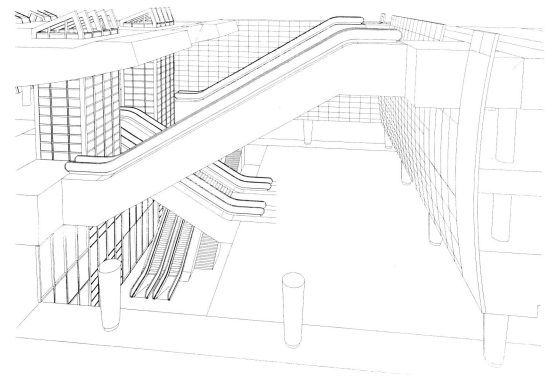

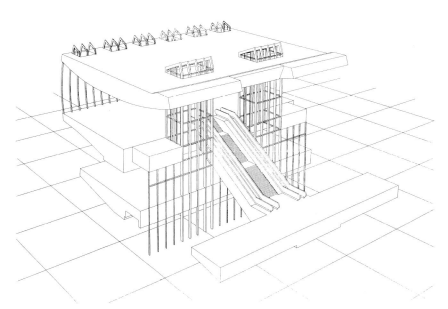

FROM ABOVE:
Perspective of the
arrivals check-in
area; perspective
of light wells and
entrance escalators;
axonometric of light
wells

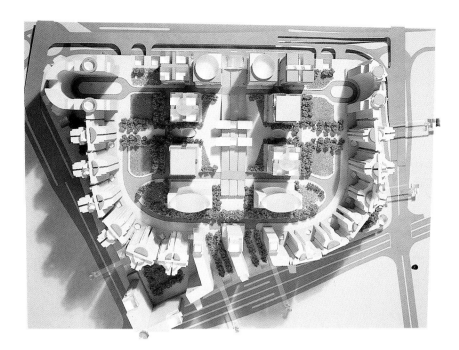

ABOVE: Model of masterplan; CENTRE and BELOW: Views of the model of Kowloon Station

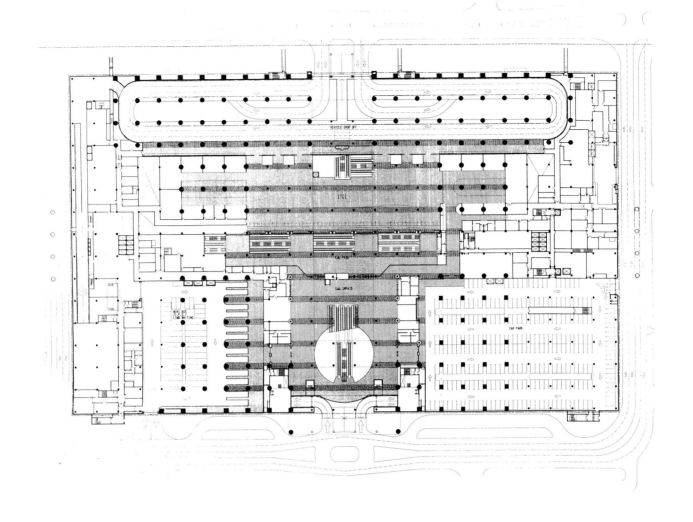

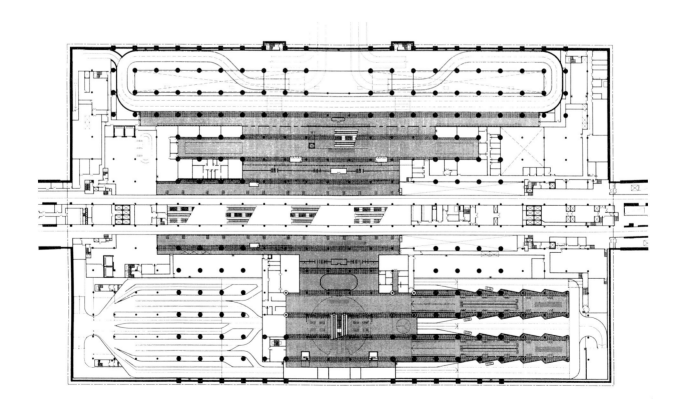

FROM ABOVE: Concourse level plan; arrivals and departure floor plan

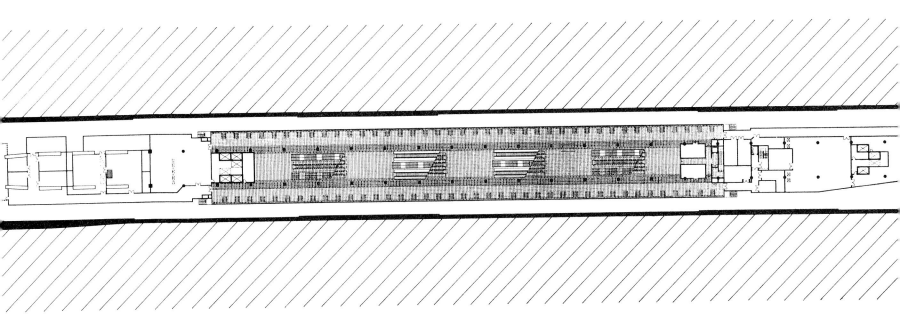

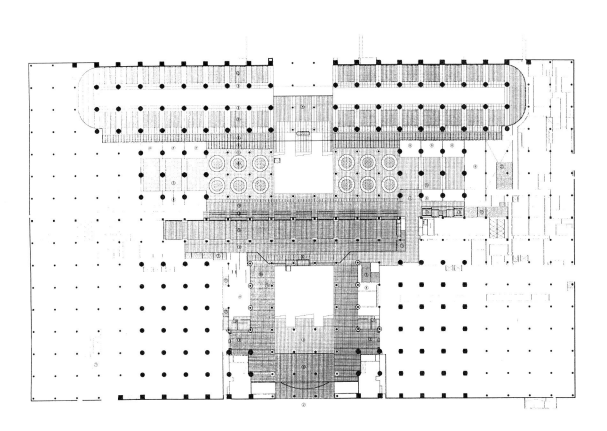

FROM ABOVE: Airport line platform level plan; reflected ceiling plan of concourse level

SLOTERDIJK
AMSTERDAM, THE NETHERLANDS

Architect: *Harry Reijnders;* Engineer: *Koos Hartog;* Designed: *1983;* Construction: *1984–86*

Walk into the glass walled concourse at Sloterdijk and you will see one of the most compelling images in the whole history of railway architecture: an express train rolling through the station above you in a glass tunnel. Here is what the French call *architecture parlante*, a building which proclaims its purpose.

Amsterdam Sloterdijk is a transport interchange on three levels. At ground level there is a continuous stream of suburban trains in smart blue and yellow liveries, including double deckers. Mid-level is the concourse where cars, buses and trams depart from directly outside the concourse hall. At the higher level are the twin tracks of the main line which links Schipol Airport with Leiden, the Hague and Amsterdam.

Sloterdijk is the first great work of the present day genius of Dutch railway architecture Harry Reijnders. He was given the commission in 1983 aged 34. The lower level of the station had already begun. 'I nearly cried when I saw what had been done', said Reijnders. What distressed him was the sheer mass of concrete bulwarks rising to take the station above. Reijnders' vision was instead, a modern day version of the steel and glass termini of the nineteenth century. His achievement at Sloterdijk was to make the most of this contrast by setting a glass cathedral above against the dark and massive substructure below.

The first requirement was for a large airy concourse hall. Reijnders created a glass box with a difference. He had observed how stations quickly become a clutter of advertisements and determined to create a concourse without columns or solid walls for anyone to attach things to. This he achieved by constructing a stylish white 'scaffold' structure from which walls and roof are supported. It is built of intersecting tubes and cross-braces, forming a huge openwork lattice, eye-catching in itself; and, to prove an engineering point, the whole weight of each corner piece descends to a single small stout column.

Internally Reijnders' station is based on the simple premise that there is no more dazzling colour in architecture than the blue of the sky:

Light and colour are two of the most important building materials. We believe our stations must be bright open places with maximum visibility. Then you don't need picturegrams telling everyone where to go. . . . You know the old saying of the modern movement 'Less is more'. Well we say, less is a bore! We believe in putting decoration back into architecture. Decoration has a function. We want our stations to be pleasing places to wait in.

Market research showed that passengers were as concerned about cold draughty platforms as they were about prices and finding seats on trains. At Sloterdijk the upper level is 40 metres above the ground – where a storm force eight wind will blow at over 110 kilometres per hour. Wind tunnel tests showed the best way to protect passengers was to cocoon them in a gently curving tunnel running north–south. As the prevailing wind is from the west, it is draught-free on all but a few days a year. While a glass roof naturally heats up fast in full sun, the trains passing every ten minutes pull a vast draught of cooling air through the station, ensuring it never becomes stiflingly hot in summer. Some internal shade is provided on a very hot day by the white canopies running the length of the platforms.

On a bright day, the station has the red, white and blue livery of a tricolour. The blue of the sky is picked up in the cornflower blue of the arched girders supporting the roof – in the sun the platforms turn white reflecting the under side of the canopy – while the transverse girders supporting the canopy are Ferrari red. The signs and station furniture matches the livery.

Where bright colours are used, it is all the more essential to keep a station clean. However frequently trains are washed, deposits accumulate from steel brakes and copper electricity connections. At Sloterdijk, the glass tunnel walls have their own rails – allowing a cleaning gantry, in the form of a curved ladder, to glide along just above the glass walls.

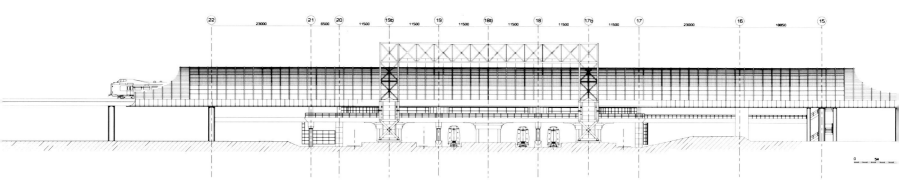

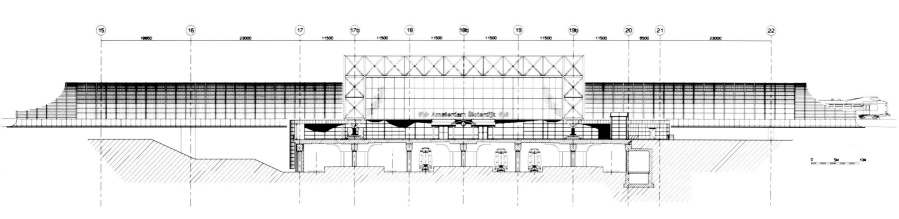

FROM ABOVE: Rear elevation; entrance elevation

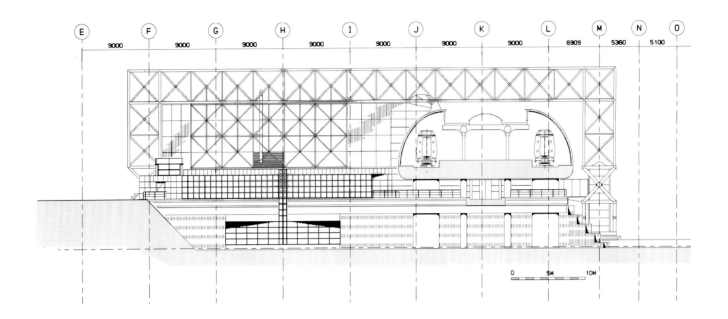

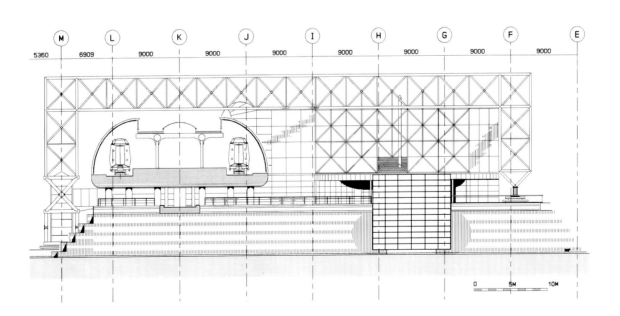

FROM ABOVE: Sectional elevation looking east; sectional elevation looking west

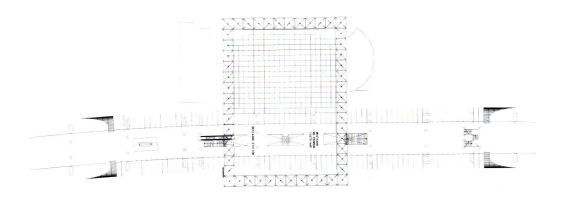

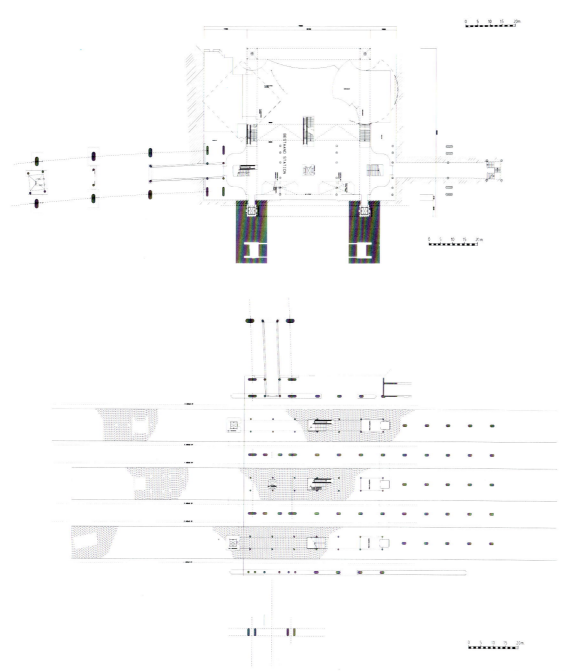

FROM ABOVE: Upper level plan and roof plan of concourse; concourse level; ground level

DUIVENDRECHT
Amsterdam, the Netherlands

Architect: *Peter Kilsdonk of NS Architects;* Engineer: *Lazlo Vakar;* Designed: *1988-89;* Construction: *1990–93*

This station is a symphony in white steel, bright by day and night. Roofs, canopies, glazing bars, handrails, lampposts and structural supports are all predominantly white, the railways' equivalent of an all-white Mediterranean cruise liner. This also serves to emphasise the few external colour accents more strongly.

The new station is at the intersection where the new Schipol Airport line crosses over the existing Amsterdam–Utrecht line at right angles. Eventually the station is expected to cater for seventy thousand passengers a day, many of them changing trains. On the top level parallel to the Amsterdam–Utrecht trains, run the tracks of the Amsterdam metro, allowing passengers to change trains simply by crossing platforms. The Schipol line below has provision to double from two to four tracks if required. The architect, Peter Kilsdonk, explains the changes:

> To build the new station, 120 metres of the earth embankment carrying the Amsterdam–Utrecht line were removed. The tracks now run over prefabricated concrete bridges with a length of 115 metres.

Kilsdonk's paramount consideration was to ensure passengers could move quickly, freely and easily. If you approach by road the station entrances are marked by huge red equilateral triangles (each side measuring 25 metres). Beneath the canopy is a tall glass cylinder announcing the entrance. The doors are edged with broad bands of red so there is no mistaking them.

Inside, the emphasis is on transparency and maximum visibility, across the concourse and platforms, and from level to level. Ticket office, shops and restaurant are situated at first floor level and staircases, elevators and lifts are clearly visible. 'A station doesn't have to be a poorly organized labyrinth or a catacomb', says Kilsdonk. His one conceit was to paint every column a different colour, following colours used by Le Corbusier and Loos. This dispels the sense of a colonnade dividing the space into two parts.

Both platforms on the Schipol line project well beyond the main body of the station and are covered by glass canopies. 'Wind tunnel tests showed that gusts of wind could be a hazard at this level', continues Kilsdonk. On the inside, the canopies have curved white roofs and continuous bands of windows, almost like railway carriages. On the other they have blue glazed hoops (like those at Sloterdijk) adding a splash of colour.

Above, the lines run through a broad, well-lit station hall measuring 150 by 45 metres. This is a technical *tour de force*, largely uninterrupted by columns. Daylight reaches every corner of the building from above, according to Kilsdonk, 'through numerous voids and via glass walls from all sides. Ceilings too have been painted high gloss white. Columns are minimal and wherever possible in slender steel.' See-through moving staircases and glass-panelled balustrades add to the transparency. 'People can see and be seen. The building rates high on the social safety scale', he adds.

Careful attention has been paid to landscaping. There are ponds under the railway bridges. One of the approaches to the Schipol platforms takes passengers across a low level bridge, with an eye-catching red balustrade, to a small island. From here a flying staircase, with its own canopy, leads up to the platform; it might be a gangway up to a Cunard Queen. Kilsdonk understands how passengers need to be treated and takes everything into consideration: 'On entering,' he says, 'you will see a solitary cedar-tree. This will grow to 25 metres. It is enclosed in a courtyard garden so litter will not spoil it'.

OPPOSITE, FROM ABOVE: Site plan; northwest elevation; cross section through entrance hall; entrance elevation showing section through upper level tracks; longitudinal section

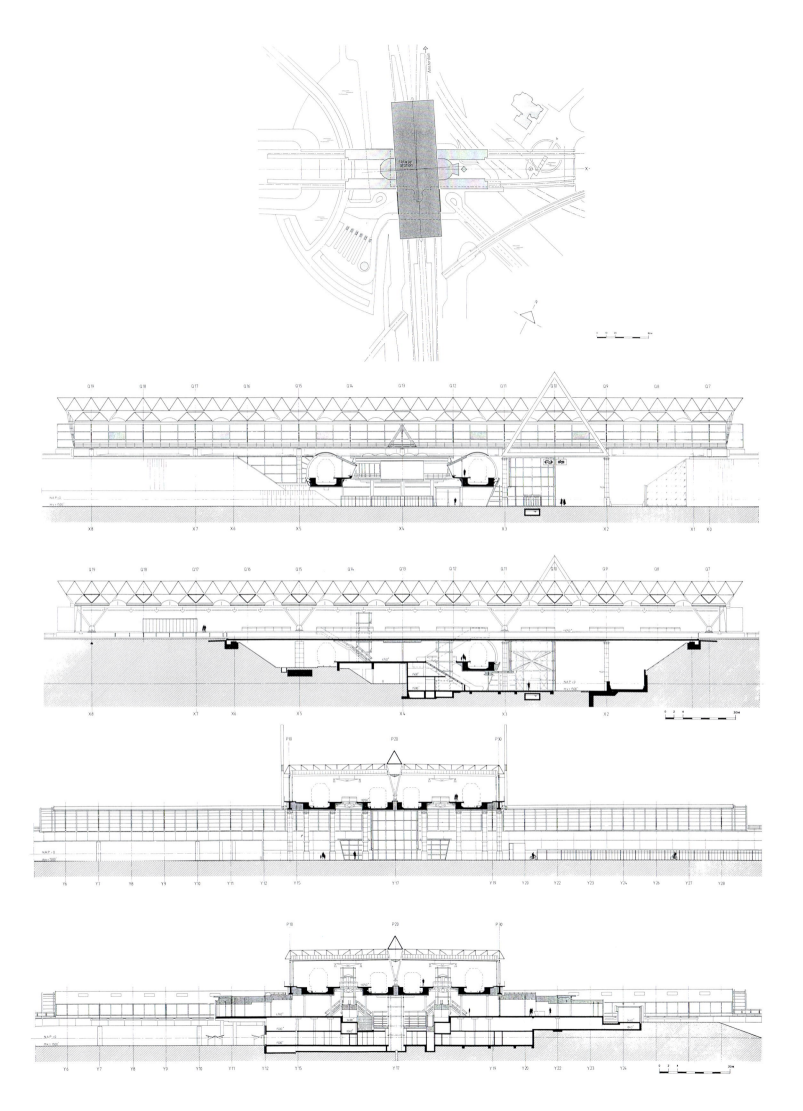

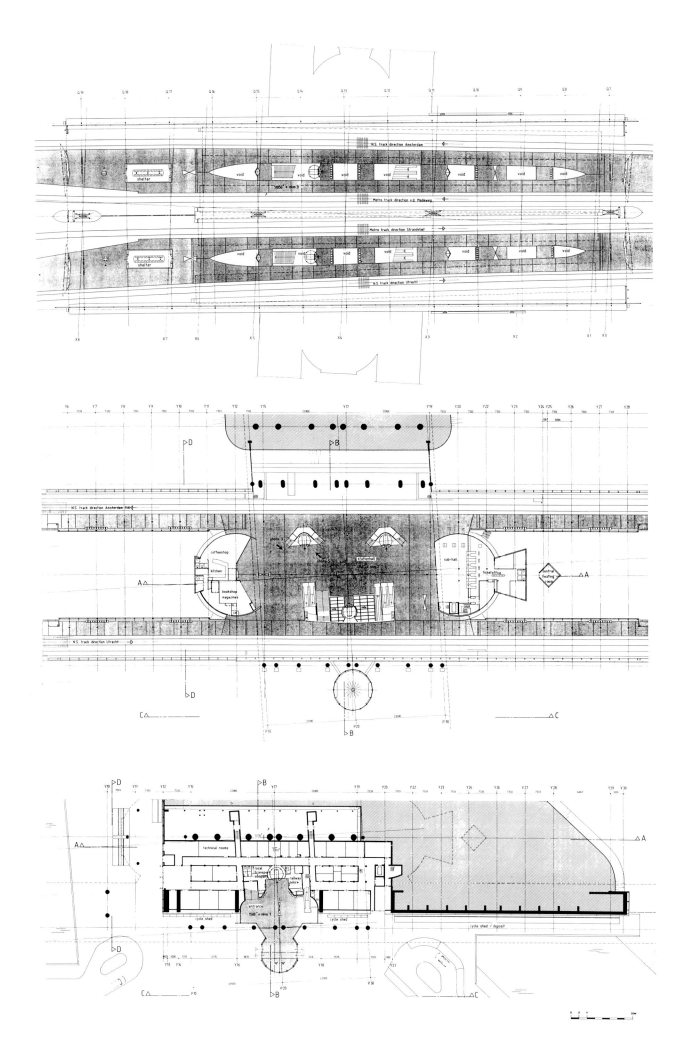

FROM ABOVE: Second floor plan; first floor plan; ground floor plan

LEIDEN CENTRAL
LEIDEN, THE NETHERLANDS

Architect: *Harry Reijnders;* Engineers: *Harry Beertsen;* Designed: *1989-90;* Construction: *1992–95*

Leiden is a thriving university city with a large and beautiful old quarter. The central station is cut off from the town centre by a very busy main road, however, and the station precinct has become crowded, confused and fume-ridden.

Statistics indicate the problem. Leiden Central is the fifth busiest station in the Netherlands. The bus station is the fourth largest. Every day over forty thousand bus passengers use the station square; as many again use the station. Some thirty-two thousand cars and twenty thousand bicycles pass the square daily while buses set down and pick-up one hundred and twenty times an hour. According to Harry Reijnders:

> Visitors find it difficult to orient themselves and are often unable to locate the approach to the city centre. Equally the railway line and four-lane highway form a barrier to the area of the city north of the station.

In the local press the station square has been dubbed the theatre of a 'traffic war'.

Initially, the municipal council had sought to improve the area through a joint venture with public and private organisations. The council owns the station square or *stationsplein*, the land behind the station belonged to the Ministry of Education and Science, but was subsequently acquired by the University Hospital of Leiden and a private company Medipark BV. The various uses and owners proved unable to reconcile their different interests, so the council decided to develop the entire plan itself, and won a grant from the Ministry of Public Transport and Works for 81 million guilders for a road tunnel under the station square. The total cost is estimated at 140 million guilders, and is due for completion in 1995.

When the scheme is completed, road traffic will disappear into a tunnel beneath the station square. Noise from traffic entering the tunnels will be screened by new buildings enclosing the square. Buses and taxis will be relocated. The square will become the domain of cyclists and pedestrians, but the cyclists too will be eased gently out of sight.

The centre of the square will be slightly raised and below the pavement – but only one metre below present ground level – a vast new bicycle store will be built. The sheer number of bicycles is hard to parallel in any other European country; the new facility will house three thousand five hundred. Peter Kilsdonk, responsible for the town planning element of the scheme, explains:

> . . . the roof of the bicycle shed will be in steel and glass. It will be brightly lit below and the light will rise through the pavement and illuminate the square at night. More important this will obviate the need for lampposts, denying cyclists the opportunity to use them to secure their bicycles and clutter up the square.

The plan provides for a variety of uses in the buildings around the square with the aim of keeping it alive and well used in the evening as well as the day, so making the station approaches less isolated. There will be 40,000 square metres of offices, one hundred dwellings, 500 square metres of shops and 400 square metres for hotel restaurant conference and bar facilities, as well as a new two thousand two hundred and fifty-seat multiplex cinema. 'The presence of people will increase both the liveliness and safety of the area', says Reijnders.

The new station will have a large, welcoming entrance as tall and brightly lit as a modern theatre foyer. Internally the centre of the station is being cleverly and dramatically transformed while still in use. The principal aim is to bring as much light as possible into every part of the station. The tracks at Leiden, as with many Dutch stations, are raised on an embankment with a narrow somewhat confined tunnel running beneath them and connecting with staircases up to the platforms on either side.

The engineering feat now under way is to transform the tunnel into a broad concourse, with the tracks running across on bridges. Light will flood down to the lower level by way of staircases and light wells. Meanwhile, the area above the tracks is currently being covered by a huge airy train shed roof, unusual as the arches run across the tracks rather than parallel to them. This will be in white steel and transparent glass, ensuring that whenever there is a crack in the clouds, it will produce a beneficial effect for passengers.

Site model

ROTTERDAM BLAAK
ROTTERDAM, THE NETHERLANDS

Architect: *Harry Reijnders*; Engineer: *Lazlo Vakar*; Designed: *1986*; Construction: *1989–93*

If proof is needed that adventurous stations can draw the crowds, Rotterdam Blaak provides it. 'A lot of people think a UFO has landed', relates the architect. Within weeks of opening it was affectionately christened 'the Kettle' after the raised saucer dome which allows you to peer down to the tracks far below. Passers-by stop and look, and people using the escalators gaze in wonder around them. Reijnders wants 'to introduce the public to the opera of public transport'. His sweeping stairs and escalators have more than a touch of Garnier's Paris Opera House about them.

What distinguishes Rotterdam Blaak from French TGV stations such as Lyons Satolas and Roissy, is the consistently vibrant use of colour. This is as strong by night as by day. The whole station demands to be featured in a sensational pop video. Outside, the huge arch above the station pulsates with blue or yellow lights indicating the direction of the next train. At night, the continuous plunging red handrails combined with the white strip lights under the handrails of the escalators resemble rivers of headlights and tail-lights photographed at night. Reijnders explains the design:

> . . . the station roof is a transparent disc, 35 metres in diameter, suspended from a steel arch with a 62.5 metre span, acting as a beacon above ground. Arch and disc work as a unit: they keep each other upright. Passengers are sacred to us, so we have given them a halo.

The concept is highly futuristic, and the round shape is a deliberate contrast with the remarkable group of cube houses on stilts nearby which was designed by the architect Piet Blom.

Rotterdam Blaak is an interchange station between metro and rail lines which cross at right angles. The metro is one level below ground. The four railway lines, served by two island platforms, are below. Both are reached by way of a huge cylindrical hall descending into the ground and crossed by staircases and escalators.

Elaborate, ingenious measures have been taken to reduce train noise. Reijnders continues:

> . . . the walls of the hall are half-covered with sound-absorbing spray-on plaster and the other half reflects noise by means of mirrors or tiles. These absorbing and reflecting surfaces alternate in a regular pattern disrupting the sound waves.

The rails are laid on a continuous ballast bed resting on rubber mats to reduce contact noise. The high-pitched noise of the wheels on the rails is deflected by hollow chambers beneath the platform edge. 'It's as if the noise was sucked into a bottle and simply echoed round and round', remarks Reijnders. Finally, low-pitched noise is damped by plywood boxes of various size, fitted to the roof and concealed beneath an undulating false ceiling. As a result of these measures, he states that the reverberation time is less than two seconds and it is as if the trains are running on rubber tyres.

Reducing the rush of wind through the station has been no less important. Reijnders explains that this is achieved by piercing the walls between the tunnels with holes well in advance of the station, so air pressure evens out. The openness across the platforms further reduces wind speed. With the help of the staircase hall, allowing air to escape freely upwards, the wind speed is reduced to no more than five metres a second when two trains are passing through the station and two standing at the platforms.

The station is well conceived for the passenger in a hurry; stairs and escalators begin immediately inside the entrance. As passengers descend, a large tile mural of a full size metro train is a reminder that the metro is on the intermediate level. Staircases and landings are generous in size to allow plenty of space for movement at crowded times. The contrast with the traditional tunnel staircases and corridors of older metros and subways could not be greater.

Dutch Railways has a policy of ensuring that platforms are bright and well lit during the day and at night so that passengers feel comfortable and safe. Here the island platforms are wider than usual, affording clear views from one platform to another for the whole length of the station, thereby maximising surveillance of the area.

In the morning and afternoon, a substantial amount of daylight floods down on to the platforms while at night they are lit as brightly and innovatively as a

fashionable nightclub. Huge circles of white light illuminate the ceiling, floating freely almost like water lilies. The colour scheme is predominantly warm yellow, set off by vibrant red and blue columns, enlightened by large panels of pale blue – as luminous as the Caribbean on a sunny day.

The effect is achieved by placing coloured lights behind clear glass brick. Where advertisements would be expected on the outer walls, there are mirrors instead and, as Reijnders points out, these are placed with the canny intention of enabling one to see round corners; if anyone should be concealed behind a platform pillar the mirror provides advance warning.

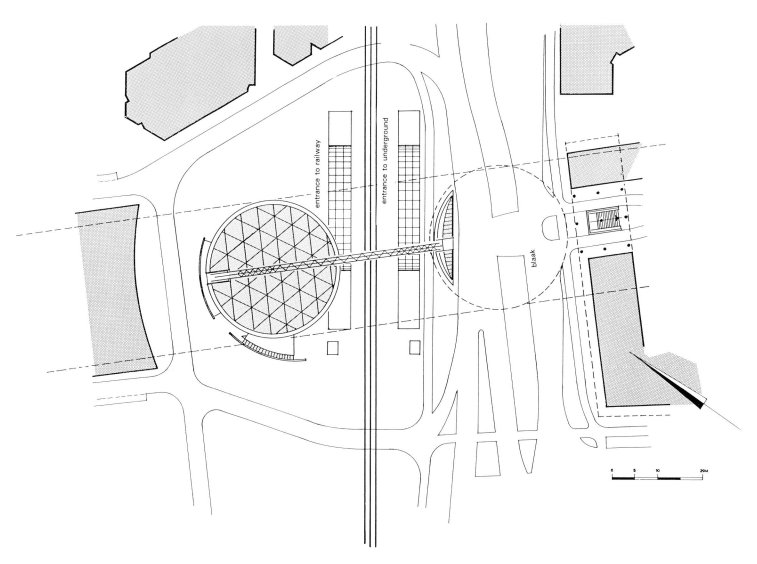

Site plan

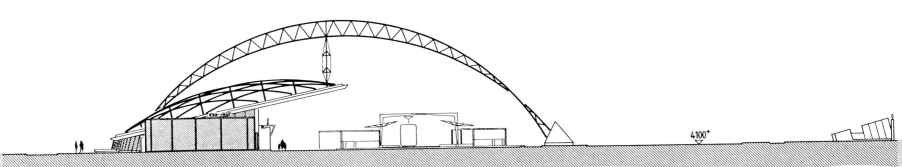

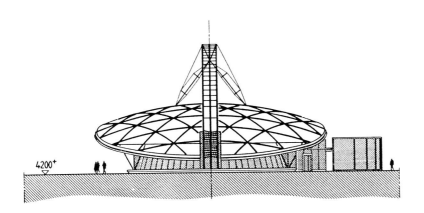

4100+

4200+

FROM ABOVE: Southwest elevation; northwest elevation

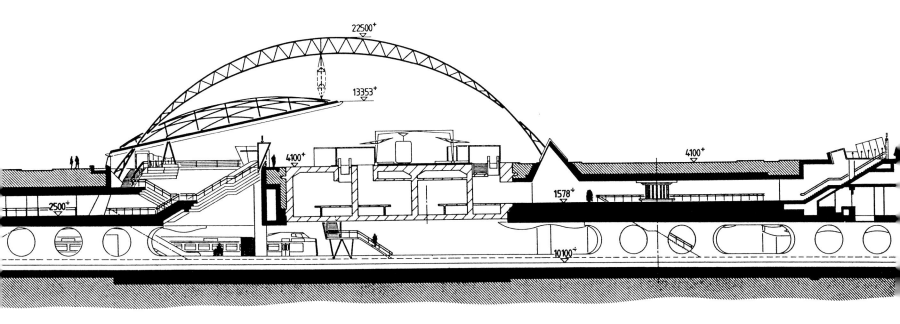

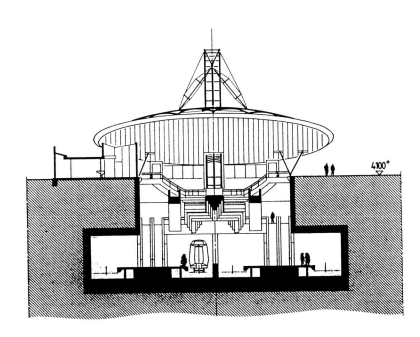

FROM ABOVE: Longitudinal section on central axis; cross section through central stairwell

OPPOSITE, FROM ABOVE: Ground level plan; subway level plan; platform level plan

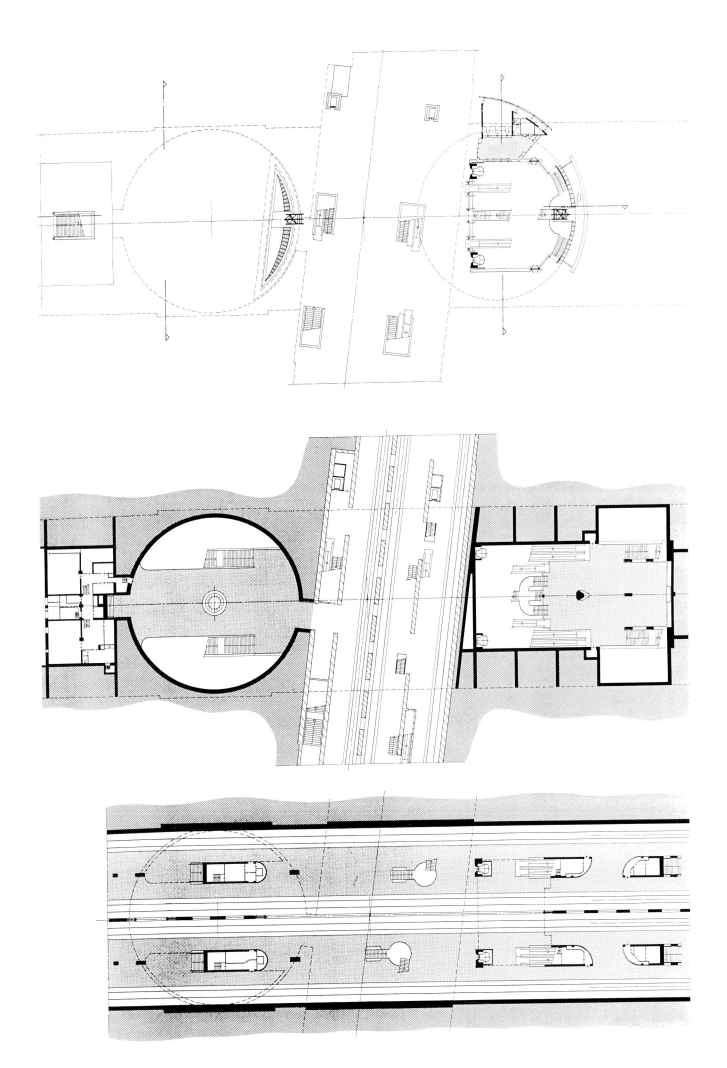

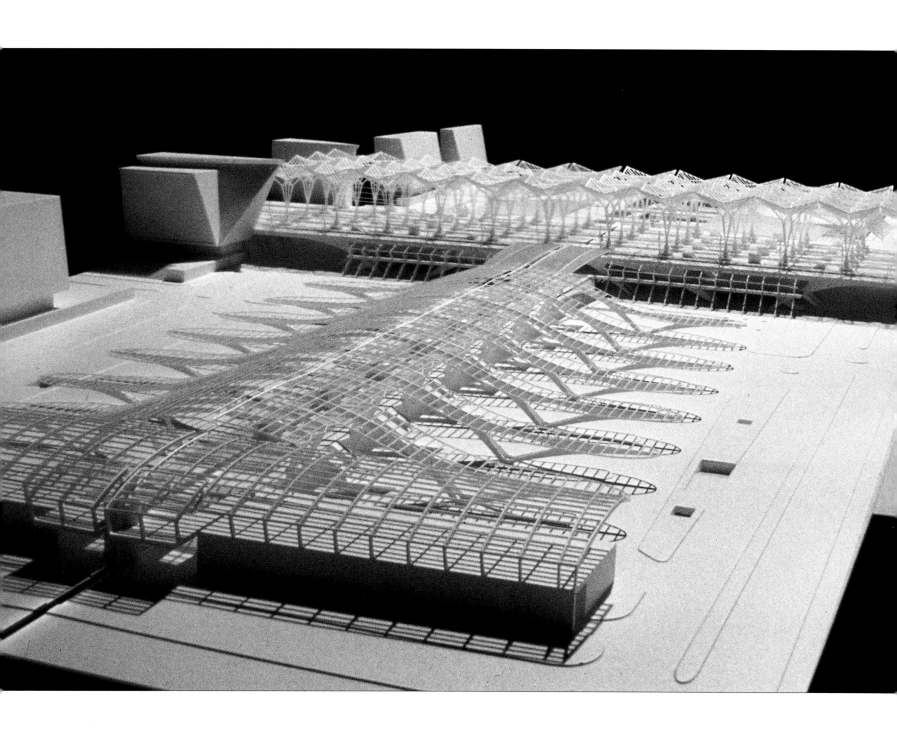

LISBON EXPO 98
LISBON, PORTUGAL

Architect and Engineer: *Santiago Calatrava*; Designed: *1994*; Construction: *1995–98*

Calatrava won the commission for the Lisbon Expo Station in a fiercely fought competition, in which he feels that his main rivals were Ricardo Bofill, Terry Farrell, and Nicholas Grimshaw. 'The key to our success,' he states, 'was the emphasis we placed, not only on architecture, but on city planning'.

He describes the site as quite a depressed area: 'In front, towards the river, is a large decaying industrial area. Behind is a very populous housing neighbourhood, badly needing facilities'.

The new railway station will form an important interchange with buses and the underground. This is not simply a station for the 1998 Expo: it will be a significant transportation node with more than two hundred and fifty thousand passengers a day. There will be a park and ride facility for two thousand cars. The airport is just seven minutes away.

The railway line crosses the site 12 metres above ground level on an embankment. Beneath it, not quite at right angles, runs the Avenida de Berlim. One of Calatrava's key decisions was to propose another avenue, set symmetrically and running under the far end of the station. Between the two he creates a large plaza, moving the bus station to the centre of it, immediately below the station.

The new station rises dramatically above the tracks, the open canopies seen in silhouette from afar. The roof is supported on a series of steel trees which branch out to form slightly pointed arches. The canopy will be 300 metres long with a provision for extending it a further 100 metres at either end. According to Calatrava the trees were designed initially to be 16 metres high but are now a little taller. Each steel tree is made of four identical vertical sections forming a simple construction of sixty-four identical parts.

In front of the station the new Praha square is defined as a parabola – a terrace in the shape of a gentle arc, with shops inset in the retaining wall.

Calatrava's bus station has dramatic cantilever roofs, projecting far out over the buses on either side. Characteristically, front and back canopies are not symmetrical; the higher, more strongly projecting overhang is balanced by a more shallow lower one. Transparent bubble elevators provide a direct contact with the station allowing people to approach the buses without crossing the road.

Calatrava's usual concealed lighting – lamps trained directly on to the vaults or canopies from within – will ensure that the station, and bus station, are also bright beacons at night.

Site model

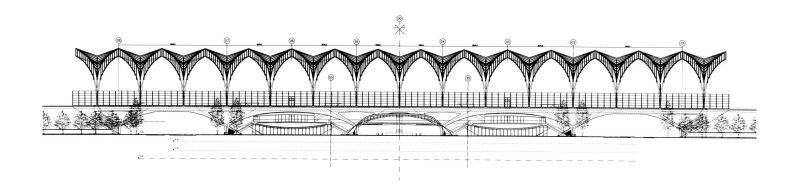

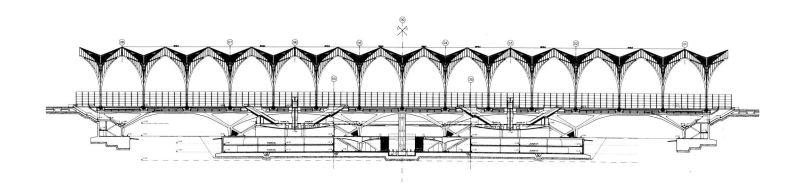

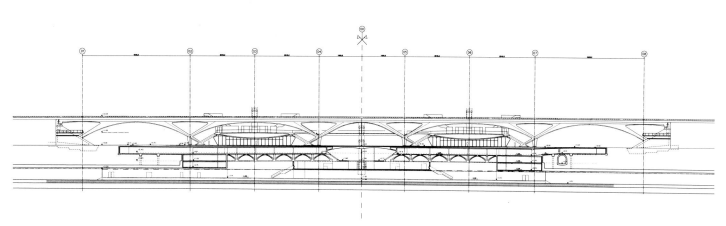

FROM ABOVE: East elevation; north-south section through rail tracks with concourse below; north-south section through bus station

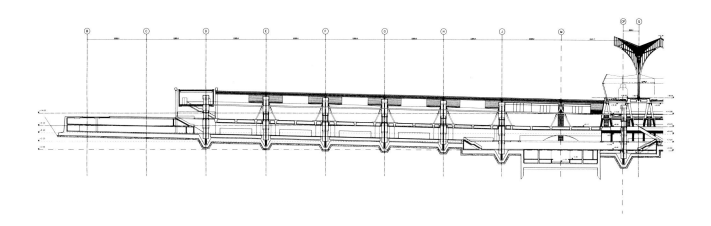

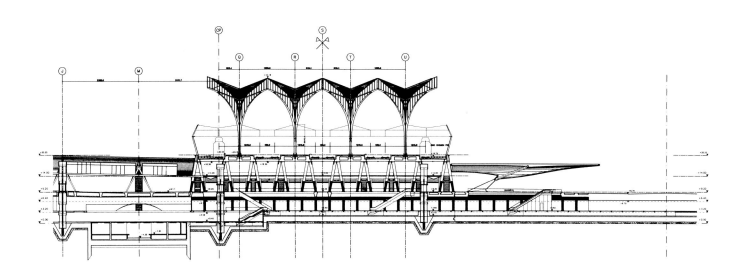

FROM ABOVE: Longitudinal section (west) through central axis; longitudinal section (east) through central axis

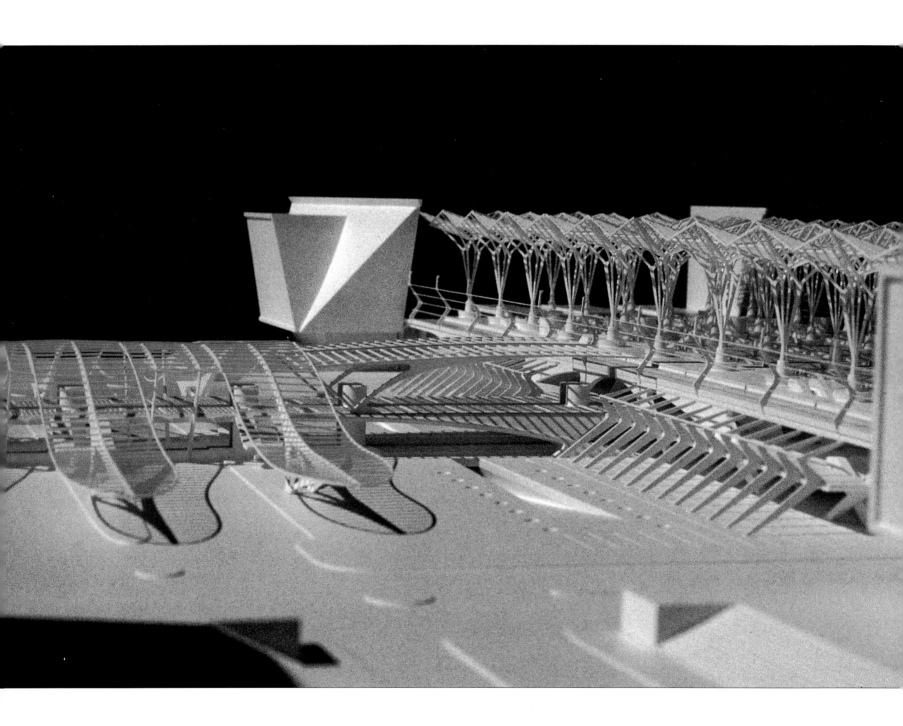

Site model

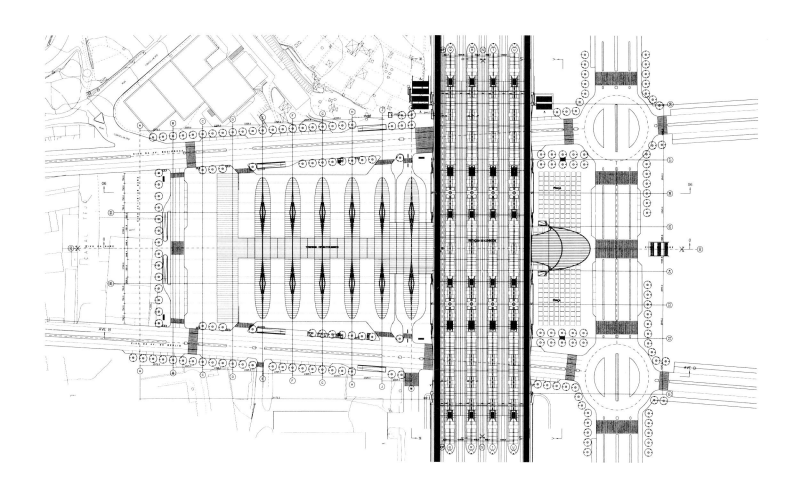

Plan of railway platform level (+20.25m)

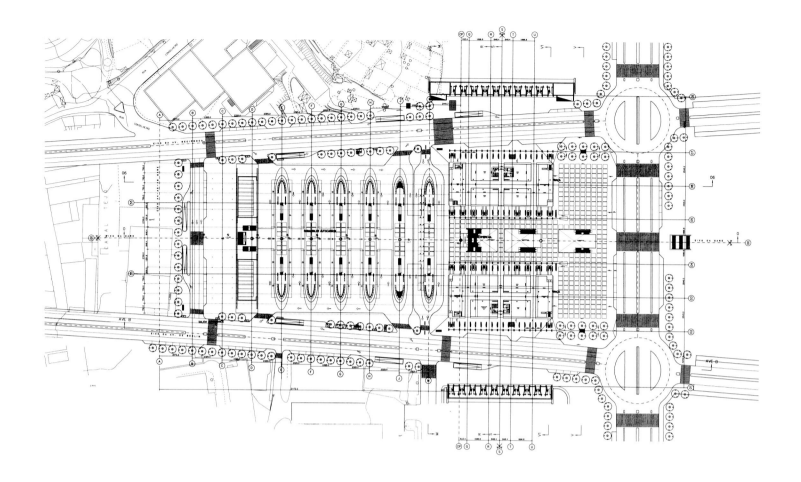

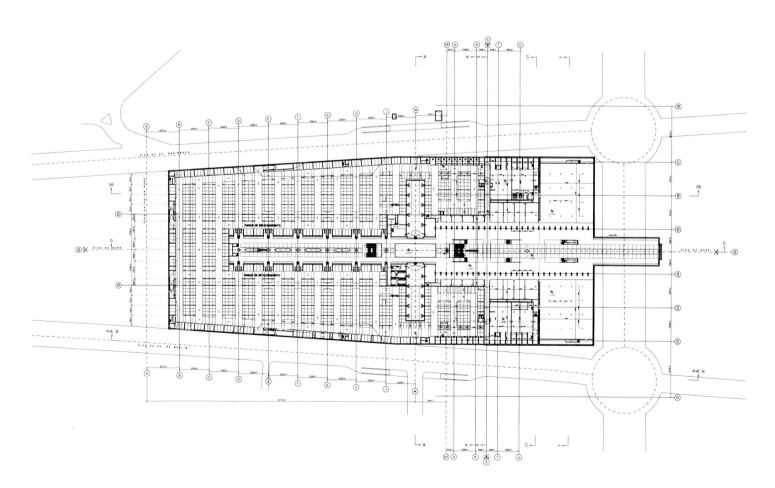

Plan of bus platform level (+9.20m); Plan of car parking level (-3.60m)

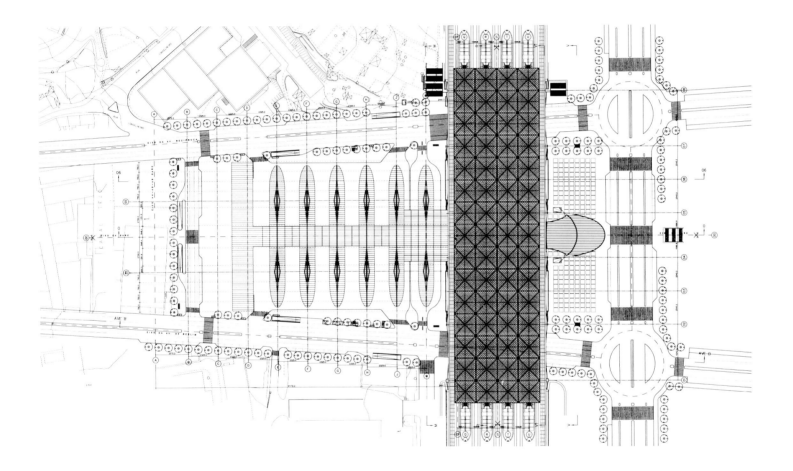

Roof level plan

ATOCHA
MADRID, SPAIN

Architect: *Rafael Moneo;* Engineer: *Javier Manterola, ESTEYCO;* Designed: *1985;* Construction: *1986–92*

Madrid's Atocha Station is spellbinding. Here is the imposing steel and glass roofed terminus of 1892 – the St Pancras of the south, complete with slightly pointed arches – now transformed into a luxuriant palm house. Today you can sit out on a first floor terrace cafe, gazing at the fine spray moistening fully grown palm trees, watching clouds of mist rise to the roof. In winter, banks of heaters attached to the roof protect the tropical trees and shrubs from Madrid's severe frosts.

The Atocha Station is an inspiring marriage between old and new – in both visual and functional terms. Beyond the old train shed lies both a new commuter station and a new AVE terminus (AVE standing for Alta Velocidad Español, the Spanish counterpart of the French TGV).

Moneo's new station quadruples the size of the old one – it extends far beyond the old train shed – occupying an extensive area of former goods and marshalling yards. Here is new architecture of positively epic grandeur. Moneo's new approach ramp, sweeping cars up to a new concourse level over the AVE tracks, is sharp, straight and steep, with the imperial grandeur of a modern day Persepolis.

His new AVE train shed is a complete break with the traditional arched roof of nineteenth-century termini. Instead he has created a columned hall of awesome height and breadth, with a roof held aloft on sixty columns placed at wide intervals along the platforms. Each column carries a flat canopy in rust coloured steel, given visual strength by a bold geometrical pattern of I-beams.

The impression is of a perfect modernist grid – an absolutely modular plan – but there is a subtle variation, not immediately evident because of the steep perspective. The roof panels are not square, but slightly diamond or rhomboid in shape. Looking more carefully it is apparent that although the columns run in straight lines along the platforms they are not aligned laterally. The whole train shed is about ten degrees off a true rectangle, giving it a touch of the drama of eighteenth-century stage architecture where the diagonal is always dominant.

The sense of airiness and space is increased by the fact that on three sides the new train shed is left open without glazing. Only on the fourth, northern side, does a glass wall provide protection from the elements. The balance between light and shade is masterfully continued in the roof where a single line of square roof lights runs between each tree canopy.

The lofty new station roof is long enough to cover most standard trains but not the AVE and so the furthest ends of the platforms are covered – as they were in the past – by lower platform canopies.

To the north of the AVE train shed are further platforms for local routes, roofed over with a large slab to create a car park. This car park in turn is covered by a series of segmental – or handkerchief – domes, which provide shade for cars. Laid out once again on a perfect grid, they form something of an engineering feat, the domes only touching their supports for one brief moment at the corners.

North of the old train shed, Moneo has created a large paved piazza. Here he contrasts the slightly bulbous curving roofs of the old terminus with the bold clean horizontal lines of the new station and creates a striking counterpoint of simple shapes. His new clock tower is shorn of any mouldings – even the clock-face is set flush with the brickwork – flat, unframed and judiciously off centre.

A second strong geometric element is introduced by the rotunda which forms the entrance to the commuter lines. Here what appear at a distance to be columns are, in fact, brick fins, with bricks set so close together that no mortar is visible. Old and new are united by the remarkably consistent warm orange-brown colour of the brick. This would be quite overwhelming without the careful contrast of line and detailing.

The stylish yet sympathetic contrast of old and new continues inside the old train shed. Twin sets of escalators, or gently sloping moving pavements, have been introduced at one end to enable passengers to descend easily and in comfort from the upper concourse level to the platforms below with their trolleys. These walkways thrust into the old train shed so that its huge volume and new luxuriance can be enjoyed to the full.

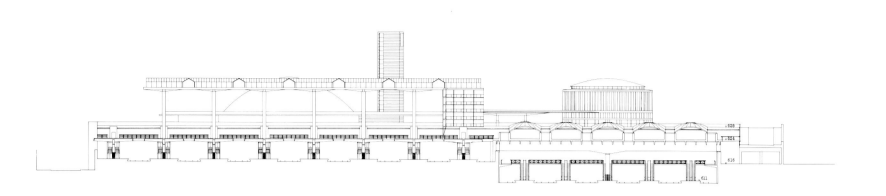

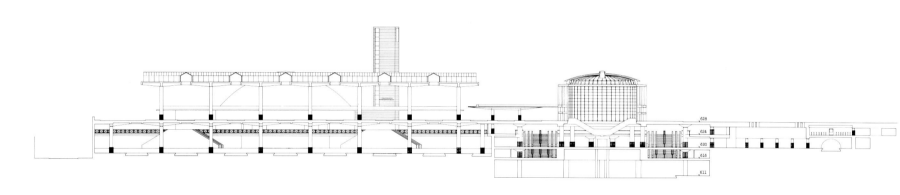

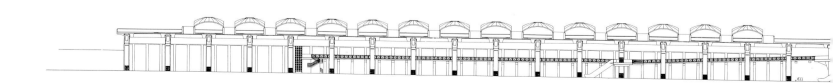

FROM ABOVE: Cross section through train shed; cross section through entrance and concourse; longitudinal section showing piazza level

The straight lines and right angles of the new galleries contrast with the curving roof of the old shed. The painted white finish or polished metal cladding also opposes the old brickwork, but as they stand free, and are elegantly proportioned, there is no painful juxtaposition. On the concourse stands an arresting life-size sculpture of a group of Edwardian travellers – perfect in every detail of dress and luggage – which constantly takes passengers by surprise and arouses curiosity.

At night Moneo's new station exemplifies the way in which buildings can be brightly lit without external flood-lighting. The new concourse is visibly open for business, with its whole length along the plaza illuminated. Beyond, strong lighting emphasises the columns of the train shed, highlighting the prospect of waiting trains.

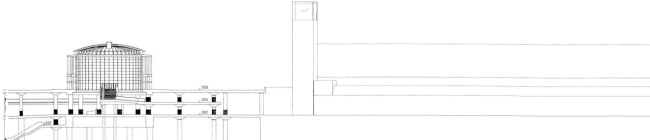

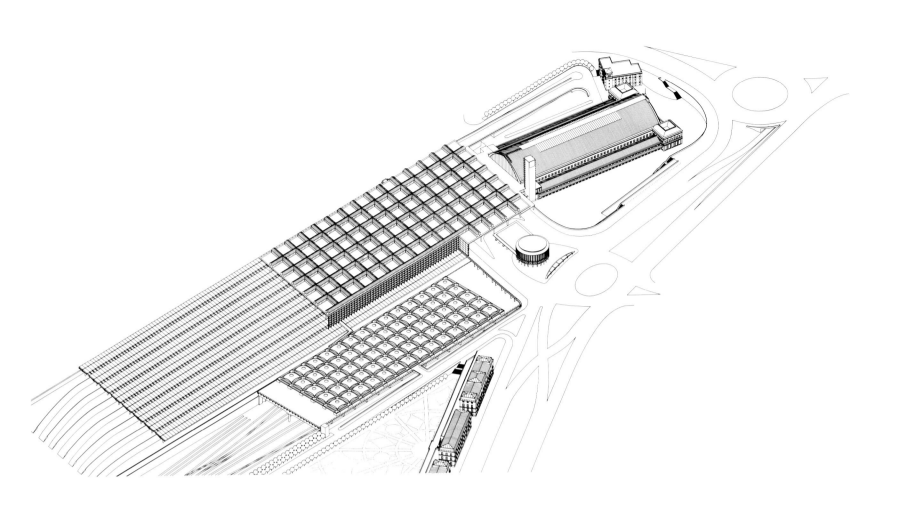

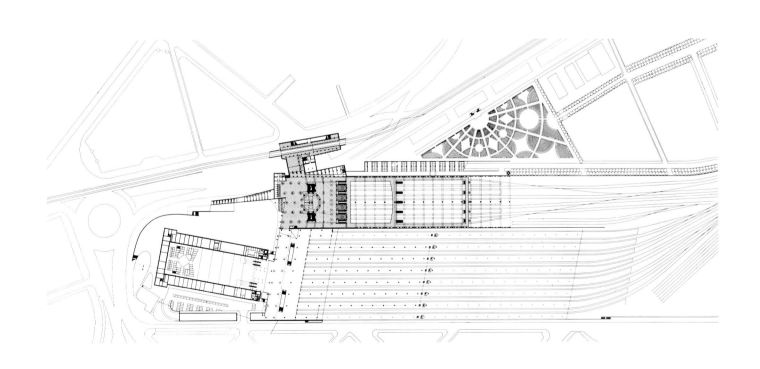

Site plan

SANTA JUSTA
Seville, Spain

Architects: *Antonio Cruz and Antonio Ortiz* ; Engineer: *Fernando Martinez Bernabé;* Designed: *1987;* Construction: *1988–92*

Santa Justa is an entirely new station built to serve Spain's new high speed line from Madrid to Seville. This line has cut train journey times from seven hours to two and three-quarters. In complete contrast to London's new International Terminal at Waterloo, it had the advantage of a large vacant site. The new station is therefore spacious, monumental and conceived deliberately as a new and free-standing city landmark. In due course, the plaza around it will be lined with housing units designed to be in harmony with the station.

From outside, Santa Justa has the character of a major city terminus. In fact the trains run on under the concourse. Its long low flowing lines have the character of Dutch and Scandinavian modern buildings of the 1930s – a feeling reinforced by the use of pale brick.

From outside, the building, although low-slung, is monumental. Indeed, stranded as it is in a huge empty plaza it has the impact of a huge beached whale. This is partly because the ground level slopes up to meet it. The fact that the tracks pass under the building, made it necessary for the architects to elevate the main entrance and passenger hall over the street.

The whole front surges forward with the canopy projecting still further, almost like a chauffeur's cap, providing a drop off and pick up point protected from scorching summer sun or winter rain. Monotony is avoided by placing the canopy slightly off-centre.

Immediately inside is a vast concourse hall, running the width of the station, with ticket offices, shops and comfortable relaxed seating. To the British eye it has echoes of Euston but while Euston is clinical, even antiseptic, this is a noble space. The architects draw a parallel with Rome's Termini. It takes its character from the clean insistently flush surfaces. The huge windows to the side of the trains rise monumentally to the ceiling. Cool grey in colour, they are set off against the white floor, walls and roof.

The architects placed emphasis on the simplest, most self-explanatory layout: 'Upon entering, visitors see almost automatically how the station functions. The large concourse looks out onto a transitional space with the trains clearly visible beyond'.

Access to platforms is by shallow ramps with a very easy gradient. This transitional space has a steeply sloping roof which is raised up over the roof of the concourse hall, allowing light to flood in at certain times of day through a continuous band of windows. The strongly directional light evokes the long shafts of sun descending to a cathedral floor, while the bare brick walls, covered by a plain slatted roof, have the austere simplicity of a Roman basilica.

The sense of solidity and permanence is increased by the travelators, which do not have the glass sides that are now almost *de rigueur* in stations or airports. They are clad in solid stainless steel panels, and do not fly through the air like bridges, but rest on solid brick walls.

The most unexpected feature is the design of the roofs over the tracks: six long tunnel-like hooped arches, which are almost parabolic in shape. Each arch covers a pair of tracks and the adjacent platforms. The roofs are of lightweight construction; metal arches covered with metallic panels. The drama of the roofs is further increased by the way they project into the transitional hall like tunnel entrances, allowing them to be seen in silhouette as well as from below. From any viewpoint on the platforms the columns line up in perfect rows.

The detailing of the roofs is particularly delicate: slender steel hoops descending to points almost like fish-hooks. In the heat of Seville's summer, shade and ventilation are more important than sunlight, so glass is kept to the sides apart from a shallow slit of glazing in the raised top.

There are twelve sets of tracks in total. Six are of international gauge (track nos 1–6) and six of Spanish gauge (track nos 7–12), with two further tracks for parcel and mail services.

When the new station and new lines were built Seville's striking and richly decorated 1920s station in the Mozárabe style became redundant. However it has been elegantly adapted for exhibition purposes and the opportunity taken to turn the area previously occupied by the tracks into a spacious riverside promenade.

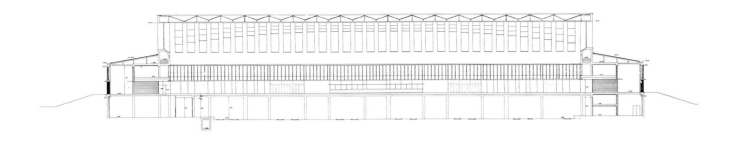

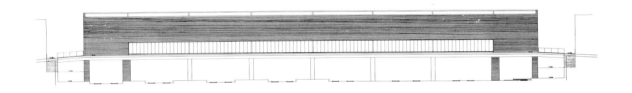

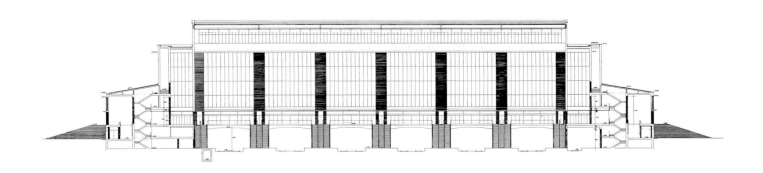

FROM ABOVE: Cross section through entrance concourse; cross-sectional elevation; cross section through transitional space

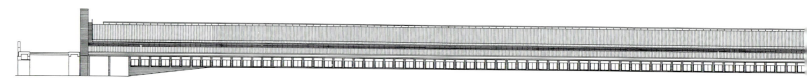

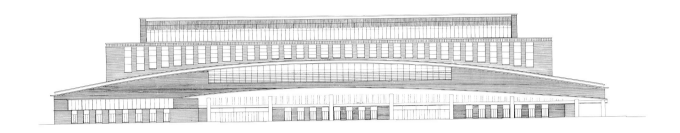

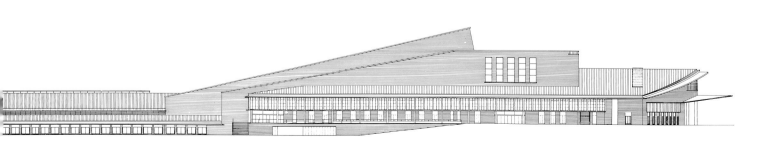

FROM ABOVE: Front elevation; cross section through the vaulted train shed; north elevation

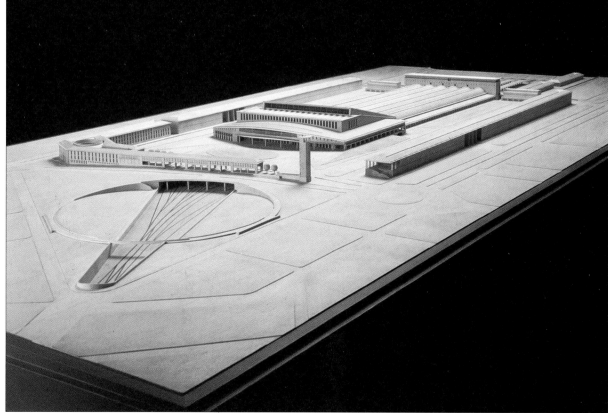

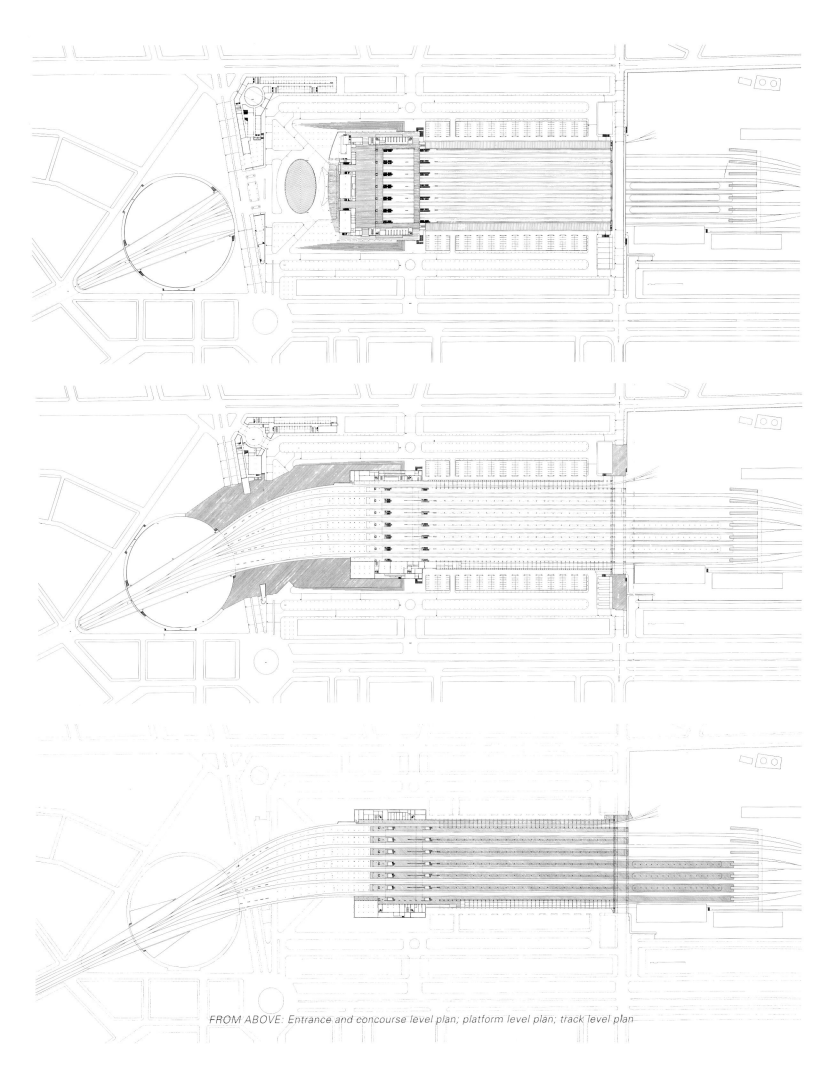

FROM ABOVE: Entrance and concourse level plan; platform level plan; track level plan

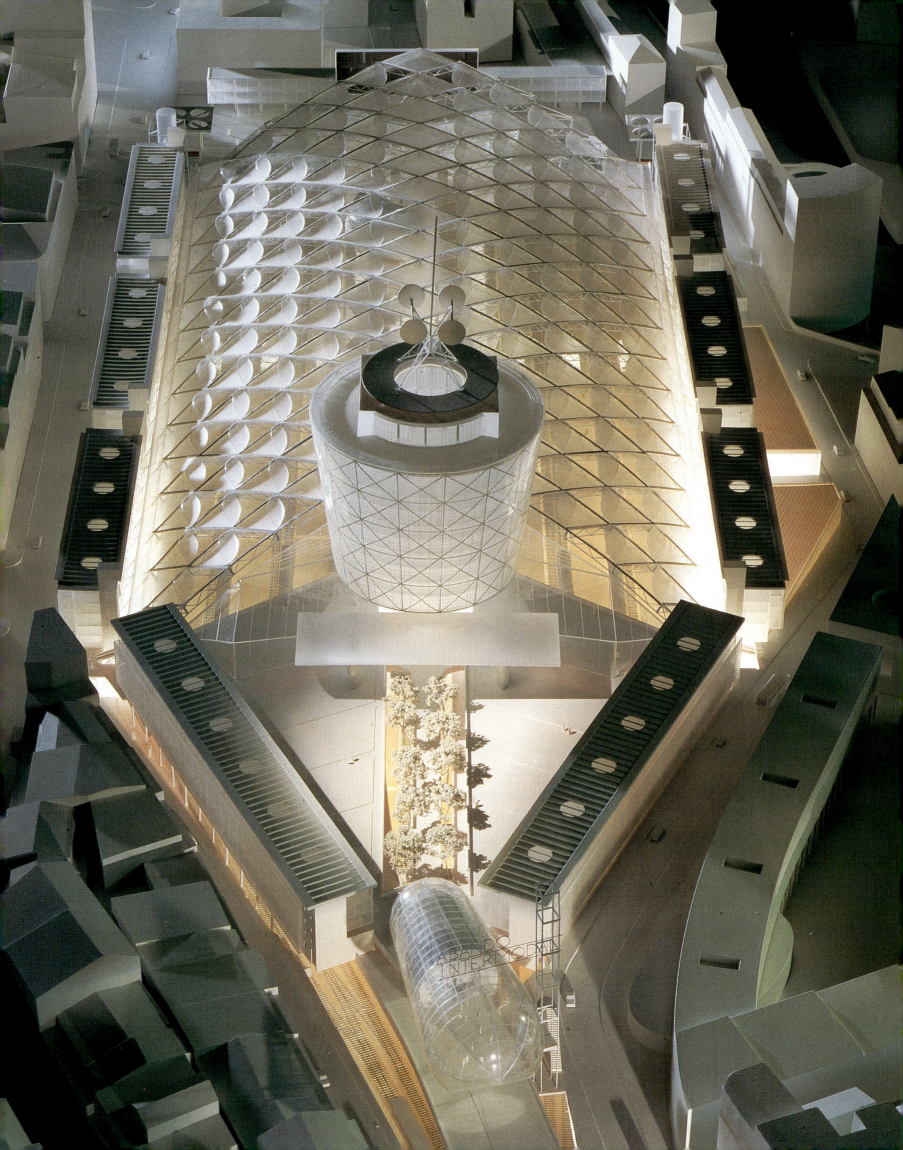

ABANDO

BILBAO, SPAIN
Architects: *Michael Wilford and Partners;* Engineers: *Ove Arup And Partners;* Design: *1990-95;* Projected start: *1996*

Bilbao's Abando Station promises to be the largest and most spectacular new terminus in Europe. The station plans have been several years in gestation and the whole project has developed radically in the process. The final go-ahead for the £265 million scheme will not be given until all of the finance is secured, including, it is hoped substantial EC funds, but in the meantime Michael Wilford has been commissioned to develop the plans to the stage of full contract drawings.

Architecturally, the dominant feature of the new terminus will be the train shed roof, with a spectacular 166-metre-wide column-free span covering twelve tracks. Instead of the familiar transverse arches, the roof will be carried on a lattice of diagonal trusses. The roof itself will consist of a series of overlapping petals, alternatively clear and translucent, which let the air in but keep the water out – the overlaps being sufficient to catch even strong horizontal driving rain. The mouth of the station will be sheltered by a suspended glass screen.

When Michael Wilford and his late partner Sir James Stirling began to work on the project, they quickly realised that the existing station, although central, formed a major barrier to movement between the medieval and nineteenth-century quarters of the city. Their brief was also to rationalise public transport in the city, bringing together buses and several historically distinct railways under one roof.

The result is a transport interchange on several levels, crossed by public walkways and with a range of facilities, shops and places to eat that make the station a lively focus of activity throughout the day. While the transport element of the station is dependant on public funding, a substantial proportion of the capital cost, probably twenty-five per cent, will be funded commercially, notably the shops, offices, hotel and housing.

The lowest level is devoted to car parking; on the next level, still underground, is the bus station. Buses enter and leave by ramps, moving round in a continuous loop. Above this, is an intermediate level of shopping with, at one end, the platforms for the narrow gauge trains to Santander. On the level beyond are the main station platforms, both for the AVE – Spain's version of the TGV – and existing local and intercity routes. The main circulation nodes – lifts and escalators – are grouped in the central spine of the terminal, and under the highest part of the roof are two further floors of offices and the departure lounges for the AVE. Being considerably higher than the platforms, the views from here will be spectacular.

As the design has evolved the great arc of the train shed has become a stronger and stronger feature, no longer dominated by the accommodation along the flanks of the terminus and the tower of the World Trade Centre. There remains nonetheless a strong play on simple geometric shapes – always a Stirling and Wilford hallmark. The World Trade Centre is a tapering cylinder – bucket-shaped may seem too crude a description – with a surface lattice matching that of the train shed roof.

In front of the terminus Wilford proposes a substantial plaza, paved for pedestrian use but with a drop off point immediately in front of the entrance. A canopy projects over this, with a cafe restaurant above which overlooks both the station and plaza.

Site location

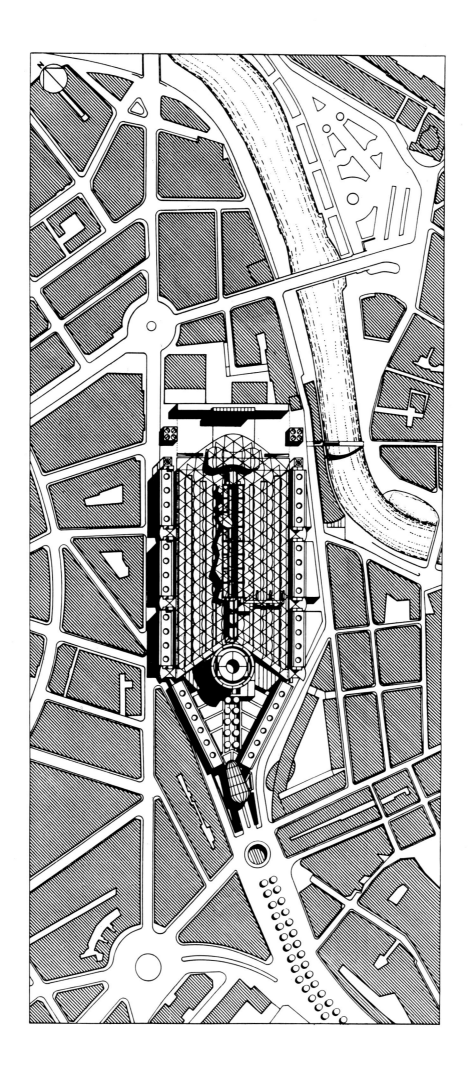

Site plan

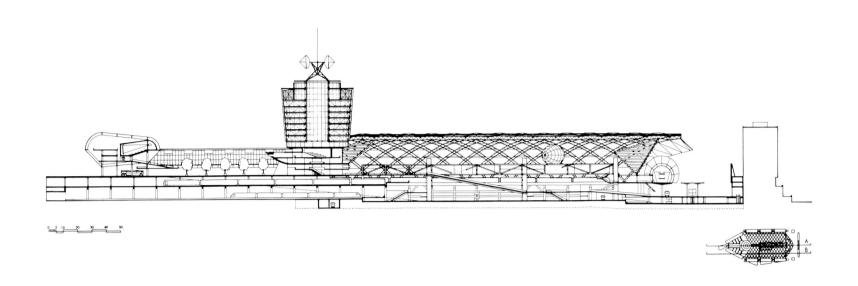

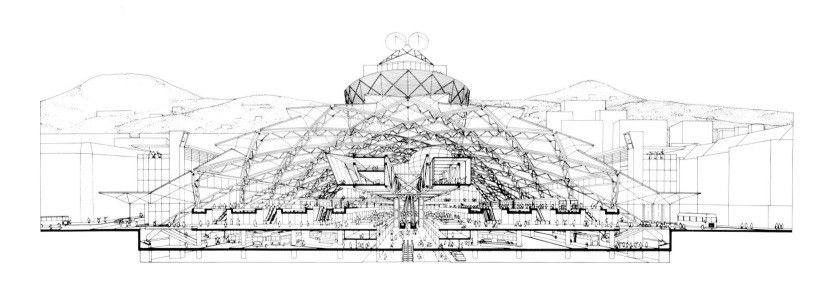

FROM ABOVE: Longitudinal section along central axis; sectional perspective

ABOVE and OPPOSITE: Site model

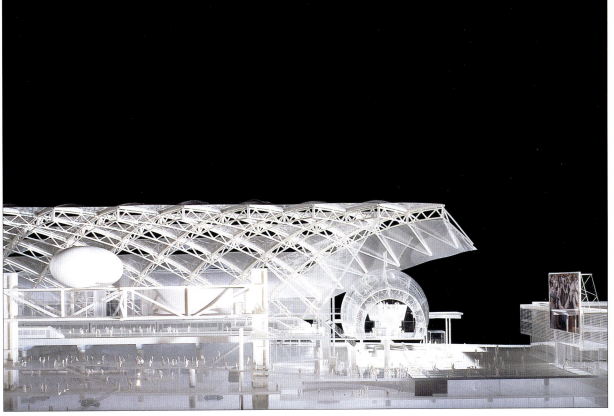

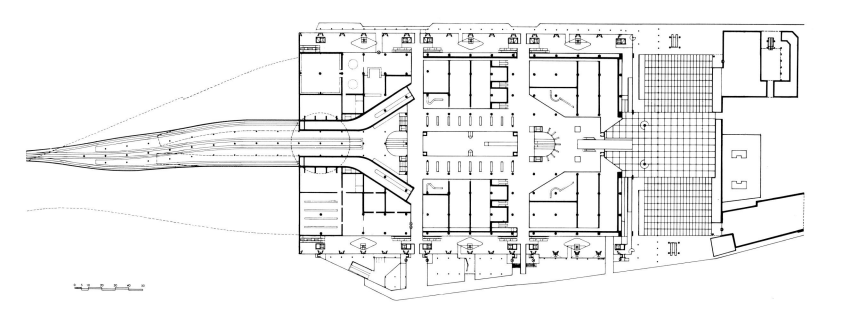

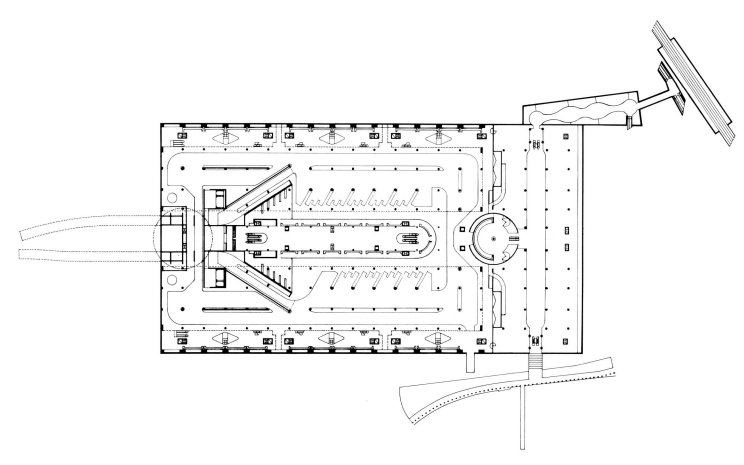

FROM ABOVE: *Intermediate level plan; bus station level*

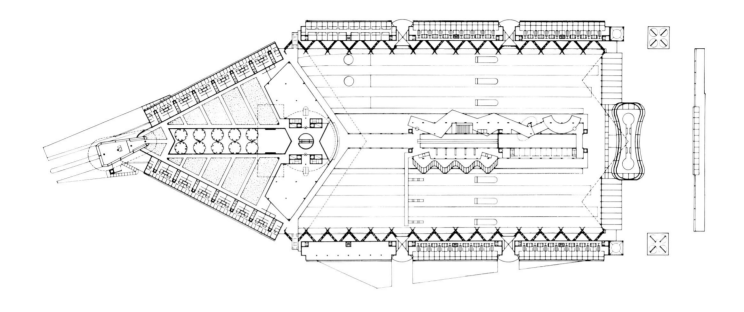

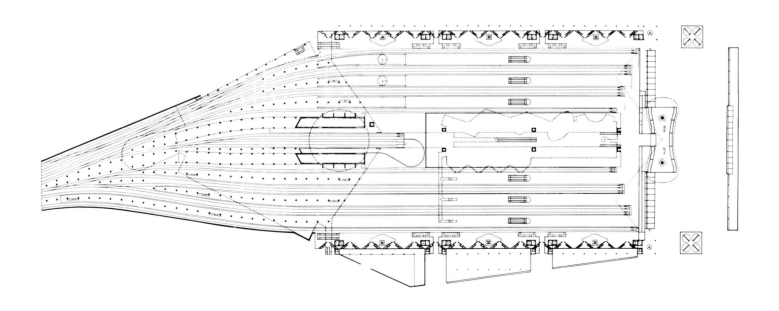

FROM ABOVE: Entrance plaza level; main platform level

CHUR

CHUR, SWITZERLAND

Architects: *Richard Brosi and Robert Obrist;* Engineers for the roof: *Ove Arup and Partners;* Engineers for the glazing: *RFR;* Competition: *1985;* Phase I construction completed: *1992*

For a century Chur (or Coire as it is called in French) has been familiar to skiers as the station where you change on to the remarkable alpine railway which winds up the mountain side to St Moritz. At Chur, surrounded by the scenery of the mountains, the holiday proper begins.

An architectural competition was held in 1985 for the whole area around the station, including associated postal buildings. It was sponsored by the station's main users, the Rhätische-Bahn, the PTT (which runs Switzerland's famous yellow post buses), the SBB, Swiss Federal Railways, and the municipality.

The new station was to be built in two parts, both under the same canopy. The first part – for the PTT, with a bus station over the tracks – is complete, the second – purely for the SBB – has not yet begun. The competition was won jointly by Richard Brosi of Chur and Robert Obrist of St Moritz. They proposed a glazed roof over the whole length of the station, with a bus deck over the south end.

Feeling that inspiration could be gained from the tradition of nineteenth-century train sheds, the architects invited Ove Arup to join the design team. A study tour was arranged, taking in London termini, Liverpool's Lime Street Station, and the glass houses at Kew.

The aim was to achieve maximum transparency; the challenge to design a structure which would not obscure the view at any point. As a result the glazed barrel vaulted roof does not descend to the ground, but is held aloft on columns. These columns, in pairs, are 15 metres apart. Snow load, as we shall see, was one problem; wind uplift was another.

The structural system of the roof is a tied arch (sometimes known as a bicycle arch) with radial ties providing restraint against buckling. Here, there is a parallel with the trussed arches of nineteenth-century station roofs. Like the new roofs at Lille and Roissy, it is the brainchild of the late Peter Rice.

Two variants of the bicycle wheel arch were considered – one straight and one splitting into two – which had the advantage of obviating the need for bracing. This latter was chosen and dubbed the *Zitronenschnitz* (the lemon wedge). The arches are in fact hollow tubes, connected by purlins which are laid lengthways along the roof. The glass skin of the roof is separated further by 'cotton-reel' style bolts. The glazing system was worked out by Peter Rice's Paris practice RFR.

Toughened glass was considered for the roof but was ruled out on cost grounds. Instead laminated glass was chosen. Though less resistant, it has performed well in similar overhead situations, according to RFR.

To maximise transparency, and to allow rainwater to flow freely down the roof, silicone butt joints are used to join each sheet of glass to those above and below; conventional glazing bars are used between adjoining sheets. The glazing bars also support the external snow rails, which prevent snow avalanching down the roof slope, and also serve as tracks for the access gantry for maintenance. All of the metal associated with the glazing is unpainted stainless steel – to distinguish it from the white painted structural steel.

Specialist engineering advice was taken on wind pressures based on local wind records and topography, but no wind tunnel testing was considered necessary and the roof paralleled others already tested. The conclusion was that the mass of the structure should be increased at each end, where peak wind pressures occurred. The thickness at the ends of the steel tubes was increased on the inside and not the outside effecting no visible difference in dimensions. Ove Arup considers tubular structures to look best when welded. Here this meant welding on site. The result is a remarkably clean-lined structure, without bolts or pins complicating the silhouette. The roof was erected in 1992.

The lighting system is unusual and was evolved with an Austrian consultant, Professor C Bartenbach. Almost all of the lighting is indirect, originating from powerful spotlights mounted on the columns and reflected off clusters of convex mirrors at roof level.

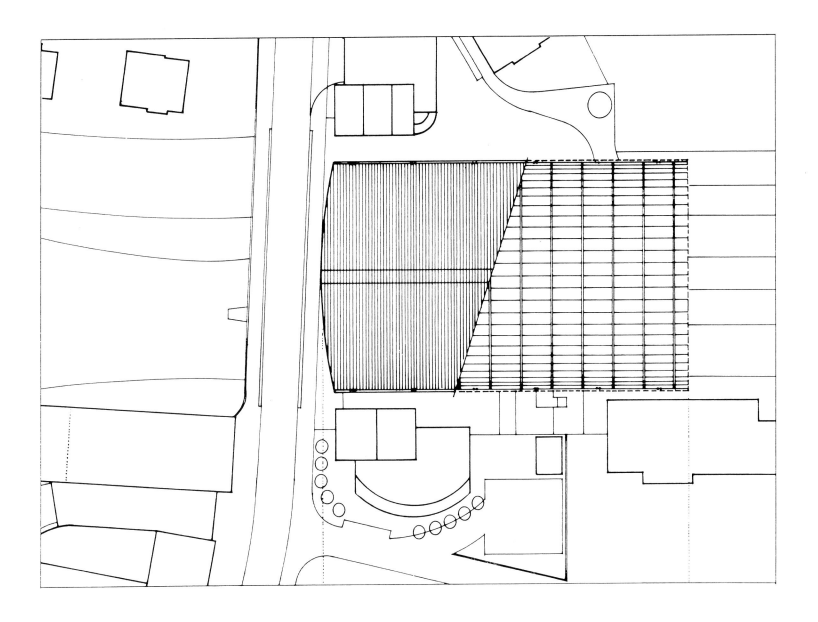

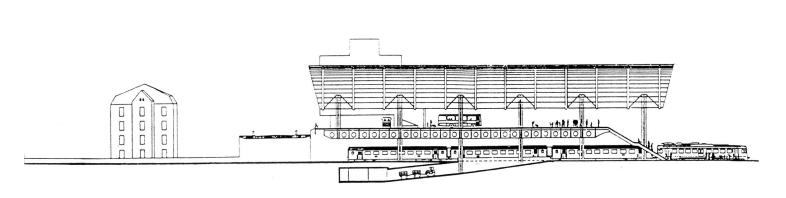

FROM ABOVE: Site plan; longitudinal section

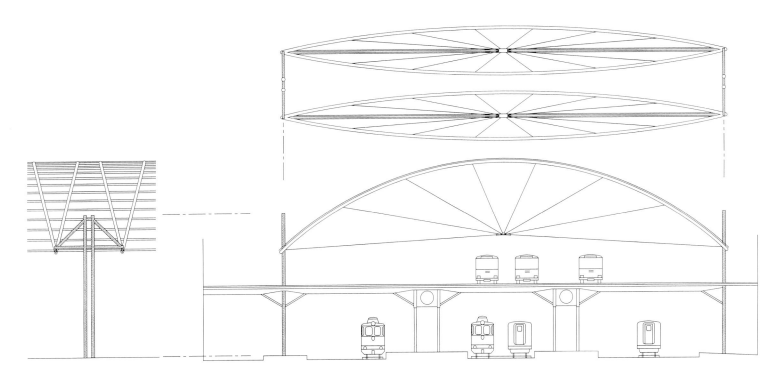

FROM ABOVE: Cross section; roof bay plan; roof bay elevation; roof bay section

STADELHOFEN
ZURICH, SWITZERLAND

Architect and engineer: *Santiago Calatrava with architects Arnold Amsler and Werner Rüeger;* Competition: *1983;* Construction: *1984–90*

Calatrava's genius brings a whole new vocabulary to both engineering and architecture, developing the organic forms of Gaudi in Barcelona and Guimard (the creator of the Metro entrances) in Paris, at the turn of the century.

In Calatrava's hands the basic unit of modern civil engineering, the RSJ (rolled steel joist) is transformed. He plays with steel as if it were 'silly putty', stretching, twisting, tearing it; testing its potential to new limits.

Just as the Metro entrances have an insectoid, Science-Fiction element, half animal, half vegetable, so Calatrava's structures have skeletal associations: of dinosaurs or greyhounds, one can never be quite sure. His vaulted ceilings suggest rib cages, his pillars are like hind legs, poised to spring.

Whereas much modern engineering is preoccupied with straight lines, right angles and compass control, Calatrava evolves most of his designs freehand: 'I work a great deal with sketches. I use squares and triangles very little, especially in recent years'. His forms are attenuated, supple, tapering, but above all in visible tension. Some of his formal language comes from that of cranes and mechanical diggers. He has a brilliant way of expressing loads, and contriving the slenderest means of support.

While Calatrava's buildings are intensely futuristic, they are also characterised by acute sensitivity to their surroundings, both to older buildings and green spaces.

When Swiss Railways decided to rebuild and expand Zurich's Stadelhofen station as part of the city's new regional transport system, it was conscious of the strong environmental opposition that could be incurred. Therefore a competition was held, restricted to architects who had already worked in the neighbourhood, and who knew the area.

The project involved extending the platforms and introducing a new track, in a confined site which would mean eating into a green stretch of hillside near the lake; the more emotive because it was the site of the old City walls. Working with the architects, Amsler and Rüeger (who had designed an elegant Modern Movement office next door with windows wrapped round a semi-circular tower), Calatrava produced a design which retained the nineteenth-century station building as its focal point.

With surgical precision the new track and platform have been cut into the hillside and then covered by a green promenade and pergola. The position of the station, which is on a curve with an unfolding vista of columns and ribs like the great station at York, has been exploited effectively.

Calatrava's basic structural member – in both steel and concrete – is a slanted figure 7, tapering to the points, with the calligraphic elegance of the Islamic figure 2. It would be interesting if he was commissioned to design a typeface.

These members are used to support both the steel and glass canopies on the south and the great concrete underbelly of the promenade opposite. Even the steel brackets holding the overhead wires for the trains are designed in the same idiom, creating a new sense of the *Gesamtkunstwerk*, or total work of art, that was the hallmark of Art Nouveau.

Part of the appeal of the station is the sheer drama and panache with which escalators, lifts and staircases are designed. Of course escalators taking luggage trolleys are commonplace at major Swiss air and rail terminals but Calatrava introduces an added sense of movement by enclosing his escalators with railings, swept back at an angle like the windscreen of a power boat.

The main pedestrian access from the hill above is across a slender footbridge which makes a giant engineering leap across the whole station, plunging down then sweeping up briefly like a ski jump. From here descends a double flight of open steps, recalling the dramatic raked diving boards of 1930s swimming pools. Intriguing, too, are the canopies over the staircases: on the platforms these resemble bonnets which could snap shut on top of you. This is precisely what they can do at night – closing at the push of a button to stop snow drifting down the steps.

Hidden beneath the track bed is a spacious new shopping concourse which runs most of the length of the station. The weight of trains and platforms is carried on a giant series of concrete hoops. As the concourse is on a steady curve, and the shop fronts are set well

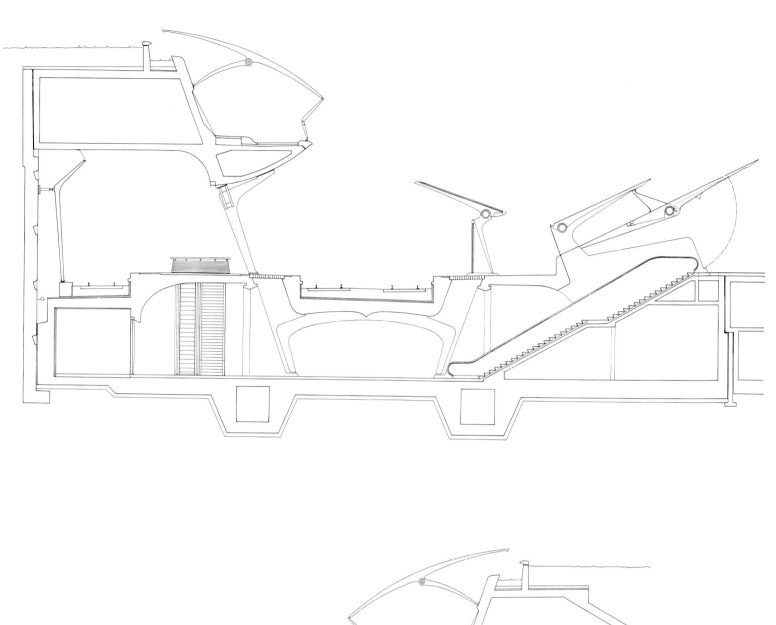

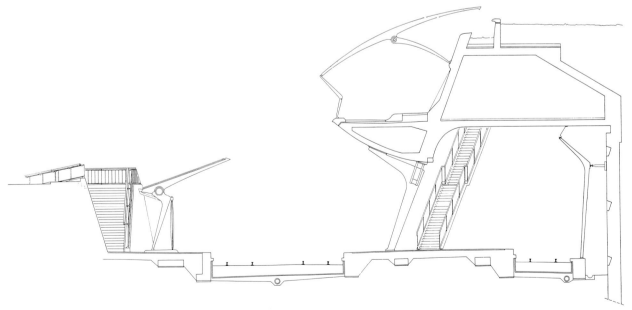

FROM ABOVE: Cross section showing staircase canopies; cross section; OPPOSITE: Location plan

back behind the buttresses supporting the arches, the impression is not so much that of a shopping arcade but a modern day version of a medieval undercroft. But between each hoop, the expressionist in Calatrava is at work with symmetrical vaults shaped like the wings of a bird in flight. Calatrava states that he is interested to an almost excessive point in developing the concept of high technology concrete:

Concrete may be out of fashion but to me it is probably the most noble material there is. My interest centres on creating a new vocabulary of soft forms, of a surrealistic character, but in tune with the spirit of the times.

At the centre and ends where the lifts and stairs are congregated extra height provides space to develop

flying concrete fins like aeroplane tails. The sci-fi element appears again in the doors to the lavatories. When approached, whole sections of wall slide back automatically.

To ensure artistic harmony, no solid shop signs are allowed: only transparent ones which are suspended over the floor to ceiling shop windows.

At the top of the station is a double promenade, half-sheltered behind an open canopy, threaded with horizontal wires to support trailing ivy and vines. Here the sculptor Calatrava emerges once more. The sloping concrete panel walls of the promenade are cast in undulating shapes which distort the shadows cast by the steel pergola, creating a fluttering, brilliantly animated surface every time the sun comes out.

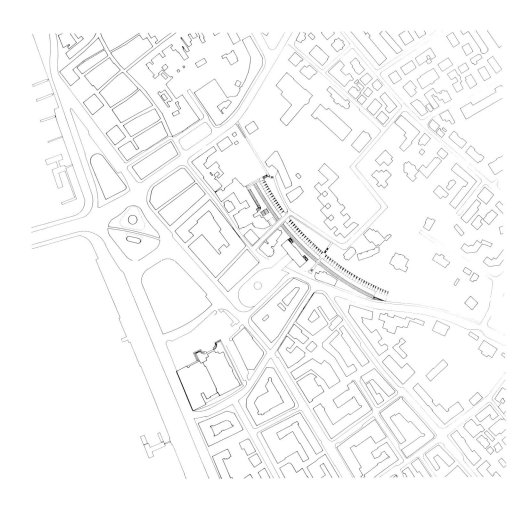

OPPOSITE, FROM ABOVE: Cross section showing the dramatic sweep of the footbridge; cross-sectional elevation

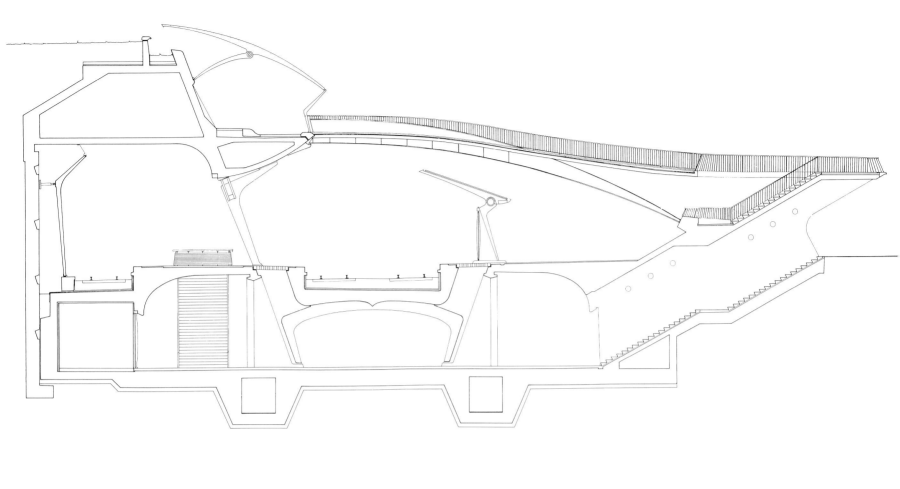

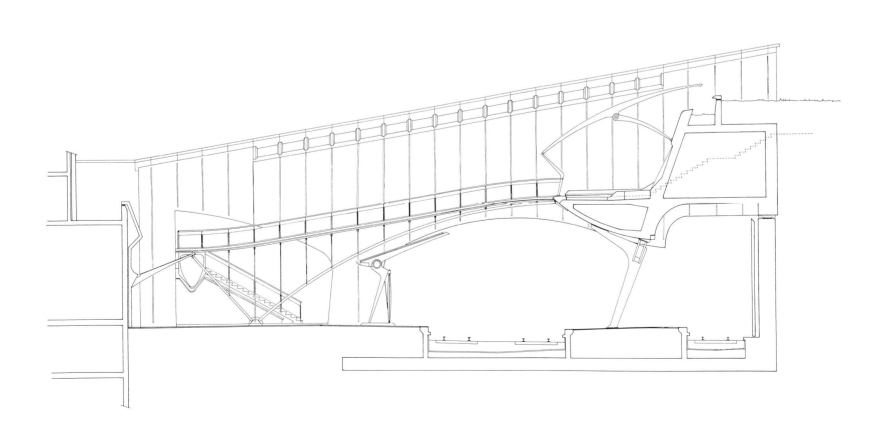

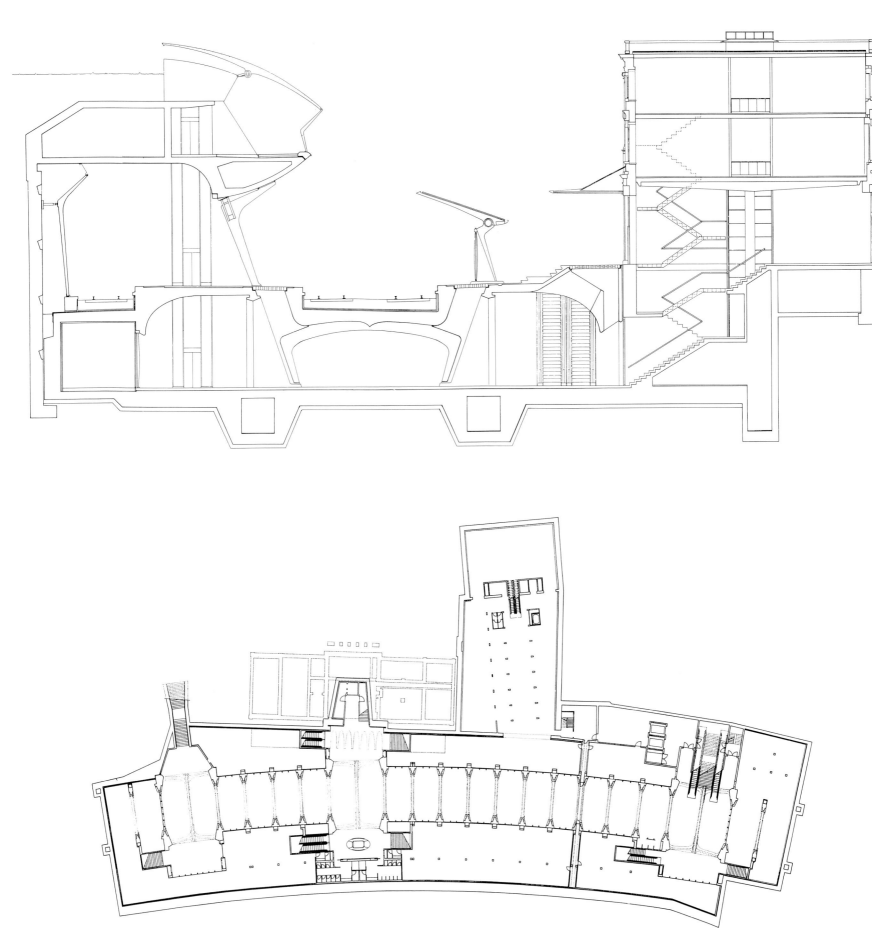

FROM ABOVE: Cross section through existing station building; plan of shopping concourse below ground;
OPPOSITE, FROM ABOVE: Platform level; roof level plan

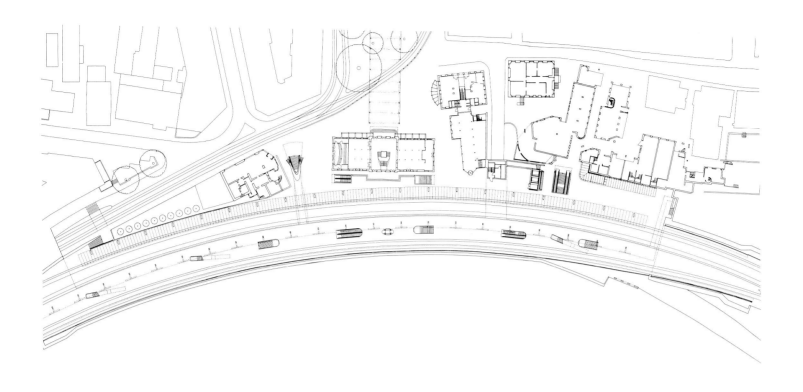

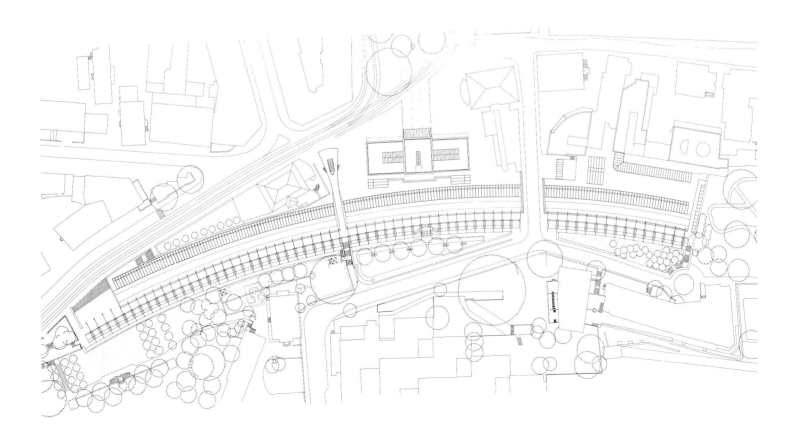